CREDITS

Written By
Matthew Eager

Editing
Carol Johnson

Proof Reading
Carol Johnson and
Lawrence Whitaker

Project Development
Lawrence Whitaker

Design and Layout
Fred Hicks and Lawrence Whitaker

Art
Dan MacKinnon

Cartography
Colin Driver and Matthew Eager

Special Thanks
John Hutchinson

CONTENTS

Overview	2
History of the Region and Peoples	3
Non-Player Characters	4
Areas to be Covered	4
History of Advent	5
The History of Hessaret's Treasure	7
Tobias & Co	7
Exploring Advent	9
Mayhem at the Wild Wyvern	12
A Plea for Help	15
A Proposition	16
Striking a Deal	18
The Company Forms	19
Into the Wilds	20
Braving the Dead Swamp	23
The Nameless Hill	26
Misty Falls	29
The Inner Chamber and the Guardians of the Hoard	32
Hessaret's Treasure	33
The Company Disintegrates	34
Nasty Surprises	35
Inside the Sarcophagus	35
Returning to Civilisation	35
Conclusion	36
NPC and Monster Statistics	37

Mythras is a trademark of The Design Mechanism. All rights reserved. This edition of Hessaret's Treasure is copyright © 2013. This book may not be reproduced in whole or in part by any means without permission from The Design Mechanism, except as quoted for purposes of illustration, discussion and game play. Reproduction of the material in this book for the purposes of personal or corporate profit, by photographic, electronic, or other methods of retrieval is strictly prohibited.

For details please contact The Design Mechanism
(designmechanism@gmail.com).

Published under license in the UK by Aeon Games Publishing
www.aeongamespublishing.co.uk

ISBN 978-1-91147-102-8
Printed in Great Britain.

Overview

At the farthest reaches of civilisation, in the frontier town of Advent, the characters stumble across a murder. As they learn more about the people involved, the motive becomes clear: One of these rogues wanted a treasure map badly enough to kill for it—but which one? In any case, now each faction has half of the map and does not trust the other. They need each other, and the characters, to put their differences aside long enough to achieve their mutual goal of finding a fabled hoard. By the end, however, treachery is assured—it is only a matter of when and how. Can the characters survive this internecine struggle? Can they determine who here is in the right? This adventure begins with interpersonal intrigue that continues through wilderness exploration and a brief dungeon crawl. The characters must sustain the uneasy (and potentially volatile) partnership while using the map to navigate a swamp, climb a narrow mountain trail beset by monsters, and find the hidden entrance to dark caverns. Beyond lie further dangers and the fabulous hoard—which may not be exactly what they had in mind.

This scenario features a pre-medieval setting that is meant to be integrated easily into an existing campaign. Detailed background notes are included for the Games Master, but most of the details are not crucial and may be altered as needed. As written, the adventure is set in The Realm, as detailed in *Book of Quests*, at about the time of the events described therein. Hessaret's Treasure may be played before, amidst, or after those scenarios, or completely by itself. Locations, characters, and historical background from *Book of Quests* are mentioned throughout this adventure, but may be altered as desired.

A plausible set-up, centred on the characters, is the key to integrating this scenario into any game. What has led these characters to Advent? How do they know each other? Perhaps they are mercenary guards who have just succeeded in escorting a merchant from Cylder, or even the Long Riding, to this place—or perhaps instead they failed and are the disgraced remnants of a caravan that was overwhelmed by brigands. They could even be such brigands, coming to town after a raid, to sleep in a bed and spend their plunder. Occasionally, a troupe of acrobats or other entertainers finds it way south from Cylder (but does not stay for long—Adventines have little to spend on such amusements). The characters might be barbarians from the Moors or nomads from the Long Riding who have left home to investigate strange civilised climes, or renegade citizens of The Vale looking to put distance between themselves and their pursuers. They might simply be local bumpkins in the "Big City" for the first time, not really knowing what to expect, yet anticipating some excitement nonetheless.

The adventurers should trust each other, having a history together that predates this scenario. Otherwise, the characters too might splinter and back opposing factions, leading to too much conflict too early. Whilst some players or Games Masters might find this a fun change of pace from dogged camaraderie, it could lead to bad feelings.

A player or two could even assume the roles of some of the Non-Player Characters, as a departure from portraying old favourites.

For a balanced and entertaining experience, there should be two to four adventurers. Just one would not provide enough material assistance or social glue—or stand a chance against the eventual betrayal and violence. More than four would likely be too threatening, as the players might opt to overpower the rogues and steal the pieces of the map. (If this were to occur, in principle, the scenario could still be finished, though in a rather different fashion, becoming more of a standard quest where players merely react to dangers, rather than face an intricate social puzzle in which they must interact with a complex group of people whilst facing physical challenges.)

Considering the perils in store, beginning characters with modest skills would probably die on this adventure. On the other hand, highly skilled veterans might find it insufficiently challenging. It is envisioned that the adventurers are in between, with skill levels akin to those of the Non-Player Characters, again for balance and entertainment. If unequal, the adventurers should be slightly weaker than the members of Zarand's gang.

Exception: A single, very skilled, very crafty veteran could keep both factions off guard and exploited by repeatedly switching sides at the most awkward moments—really good fun and challenging even for a champion. To see how this could go, watch *A Fistful of Dollars* or *Yojimbo*.

The characters are assumed to be humans, like all of the other persons in the scenario, but they need not be. They also need not be of any particular religion or culture; anyone, really, might turn up in a town like Advent.

In terms of skills and character archetypes, Athletics, Survival, and skill at arms will be valuable, so rogues, scouts, rangers, trackers, and hunters would be natural choices. A thief or acrobat would also be well prepared. At least one character should know the Healing skill. It would help to have at least one character be from the region and with good scores in Locale and Customs.

It is assumed that all characters speak variants of the same Native Tongue as the civilised folk of the frontier, though they may be from different cultures. Even Arkannad's people speak a dialect of this language. If the language situation is more complex, adjust the skills of the Non-Player Characters as warranted.

As this scenario is set in The Realm, magic is scarce. In another setting, in which, for example, Folk Magic is ubiquitous and almost everyone knows a couple of spells, the Non-Player Characters should be augmented.

History of the Region and Peoples

Two centuries ago, following the fall of Chandanar the Mad, civilised settlers from The Vale finally pushed south along the River Cylder far enough to encroach on the lands long occupied by the Grestet barbarian clan. Initial tension and conflict yielded in time to an uneasy truce, yet slowly but surely the settlers claimed more and more land, farming the better lands and grazing herd beasts on the sparser plains. Two generations later, the Grestet were once again at war, but this time the northerners were legion and had established a permanent military presence in Advent. Though the barbarians fought bravely, their number dwindled, and they faced not merely eviction, but extermination.

At this time, the clan champion Hessaret rose up and inspired his people to fight to the last. A successful campaign of raiding and destruction filled the Grestet with new hope. Season after season, the wily warrior and his followers terrorised travellers and settlers alike. They were masters of the quick strike, descending like a cloudburst and evaporating like mist. The civilised folk lost their wealth, homes, and lives to this "Black Scourge of the Frontier", and cried out to their king for aid. The garrison at Advent was fortified, but the raiders continued to harry the colonists to stalemate.

Hessaret famously loved Bōdda, daughter of the shaman Mōdant, and their union strengthened the clan. She fought bravely beside him, but finally was slain in an ambush. For an entire moon, Hessaret howled his mourning, until his pain and hatred had transformed him, and his quest turned from terrorising and expelling the northerners to destroying them. Attacks were redoubled, entire villages razed, and the roads rendered impassable. Again the king intervened, sending a great host to Advent as winter deepened. In the bitter cold, Hessaret led his warriors across the frozen river

Non-Player Characters

- Tobias: An unscrupulous, manipulative, and ambitious rogue who poisons his gang boss Zarand to get a treasure map.
- Arkannad: An antisocial and superstitious but skilful barbarian explorer, still allied with Tobias.
- Finiel: A close friend of Zarand's, a selfish but personable thief who holds half of the map and wants to avenge Zarand's murder.
- Loram the Large: An intimidating but ungainly warrior, and surprisingly honourable guy for this crew, currently allied with Finiel.

Statistics and detailed descriptions of these Non-Player Characters are presented at the end of the scenario. The Games Master should be fully familiar with these personalities to understand how this scenario might play out.

Key Points/Timeline

1. The adventurers explore Advent.
2. They meet Zarand at the Wild Wyvern tavern and are there when he is murdered.
3. The adventurers meet Finiel, who pleads for their help.
4. Tobias tells them about the legend of the hoard and the map.
5. The adventurers try to persuade Finiel and Loram to cooperate with Tobias.
6. The three groups meet at Advent Bridge and depart for the Wilds.
7. The company follows the first half of the map through Dead Swamp to find Hessaret's final campsite.
8. The company follows the second half of the map to scale the Nameless Hill and reach Misty Falls.
9. They find the caverns and traverse the Outer Chamber and Passage to the Pit.
10. At last, they enter the Inner Chamber to find the treasure and its guardians.
11. The company disintegrates.
12. Survivors descend the hill and return to civilisation.

Areas to be Covered

- Advent: A gritty outpost of civilisation, close to the wilderness where the treasure was cached long ago.
- The Wild Wyvern tavern: The dubious establishment where gang leader Zarand meets with a foul end.
- A wooded area outside of Advent, off the main road: Finiel and Loram are holed up here whilst they try to figure out what to do.
- Advent Bridge: The designated meeting place for the three groups.
- The Wilds south of Advent: Where the mapped trail begins, beyond even the fringe of civilisation.
- The Dead Swamp: An unpleasant and dangerous place, with snakes and swamp devils.
- Hessaret's final campsite: A dry, haunted spot in the midst of the swamp, where the company can spend the night—and get spooked.
- The Nameless Hill: Here a steep, narrow trail leads to Misty Falls and an attack by a wyvern (or two).
- Misty Falls: A natural wonder where the trail abruptly ends.
- The caverns behind the waterfall: The Outer Chamber holds lots of water, plus bats. A Passage then leads to a deadly Pit Trap, which must be passed to proceed to the Inner Chamber.
- The Inner Chamber: This room, with just one way in and out, holds the treasure and its guardians.

to sack the town by surprise—but the reinforcements had already arrived.

The terrible Battle of Advent that ensued claimed most of the northern soldiers and all of the barbarian marauders. Broken and defenceless, Mōdant and the last of his people withdrew from their homeland to seek shelter to the west and north, where other clans subjugated and assimilated them, and the Grestet were no more.

History of Advent

Advent began as merely a garrison of soldiers assigned to protect the local villages, and to monitor and defend the bridge over which the Great Road passes to parts east. Nomads and barbarians bring exotic natural products, such as medicinal plants, foods, rare wood and stones, spices, and luxury pelts from sources only they know to trade for metal goods and other manufactured niceties. The exotic goods from the east then pass north to The Vale, to those who can afford them. A few civilised merchants with friends amongst the wilder peoples also venture east with their wares. This trade route to the Long Riding continues to be valuable, so The Vale maintains Advent Being at the absolute geographical and political limit of control, though, the settlement has developed in a rather haphazard and organic manner, and the garrison lacks the vigorous discipline found in better controlled regions. Advent is not an entirely lawless place, but for as long as most of its citizens can remember they have been left to their own devices, with minimal assistance (or interference) from the larger society. As long as the way east remains open and safe enough, those who rule are content to let the place be.

When the need arose 160 years ago, the king's army established a simple fort, first with a hastily built wooden watchtower that over the years was converted to a stone watchtower on the low rise overlooking the bridge. A smaller tower was likewise erected at the riverbank to control the crude drawbridge constituting the final span of Advent Bridge. Travellers using the bridge are questioned routinely. Civilised folk who do not appear destitute (subject to negotiation...) are charged a toll of one Penny per head plus one Founder per wagon, but the uncivilised are not charged—a concession to promote neighbourly relations and reduce violence. If trouble arises, the handful of guards at the river raise the drawbridge and signal for help from the fort. These few fighters, operating in three shifts daily, can defend this well-planned spot for an hour or more, until their missiles have been exhausted and reinforcements from the fort have arrived. If needed, the watchers at the fort can also dispatch couriers to Cylder, which can be reached in half a day of hard riding, to signal a greater threat. This proven strategy has worked well in many (though not all) attacks.

The River Cylder is deep, its banks steep, and its current strong and swift. During some seasons, it verges on white-water. There are no good spots to ford the Cylder for many kilometres on either side of Advent. Trying to cross without using Advent Bridge is so dangerous that the river is an effective natural barrier to attacks from the south. (River traffic between Advent and The Vale has likewise been stymied, the overland route being preferred almost exclusively.) Considering also the view from the watchtower on the hill in town, soldiers do not patrol the far side of the river. This strategy allows them to focus all of their resources efficiently to guard their own side of the river against frequent but minor barbarian raids from the North. Now and then civilised bandits plague the Great Road leading to Cylder and must be handled as well. It is still demanding to be a soldier in Advent, though nowhere near as dangerous as in the past.

The original garrison of two dozen was optimistically intended to be self-sufficient, with soldiers and their minimal support crew obtaining their own food, water, and firewood. The pressure of constant defence soon showed that this busywork was too onerous and distracting, so the commander was granted power of taxation to obtain necessities from the nearby hamlets. This was met with grumbling, but the most enterprising villagers made a virtue of necessity and relocated outside the fort, where they could not only supply the soldiers more conveniently but also enjoy better protection, plus access to travellers. In half a generation's time, this entourage grew from a handful to dozens of supporters, becoming a ramshackle village surrounding the fort. As the village prospered and gradually expanded into a town, it drew more attention from traders and bandits alike, thus the number of troops was increased, the keep and outbuildings constructed, and an outer palisade erected of local timber. Outside the town, west of the river, the countryside between Advent and Cylder was developed, with farms and pastures to meet the ever-growing need to feed this incipient city.

Following the climactic Battle of Advent and exodus of the Grestet rabble, affairs became much safer and easier for the residents of Advent and the surrounding countryside. The flow of trade increased while the number of troops needed actually decreased, and the town sprawled even wider, developing in fits and starts as dictated by circumstance. Now with nearly 3000 people (and only three-score soldiers), Advent is nearly a small city, though without civic planning it still lacks features one might expect of such a place, such as large temples, merchant guilds led by master craftsmen, or colleges of learned scholars. Even its underworld is petty and not fully formed, as the characters will soon see.

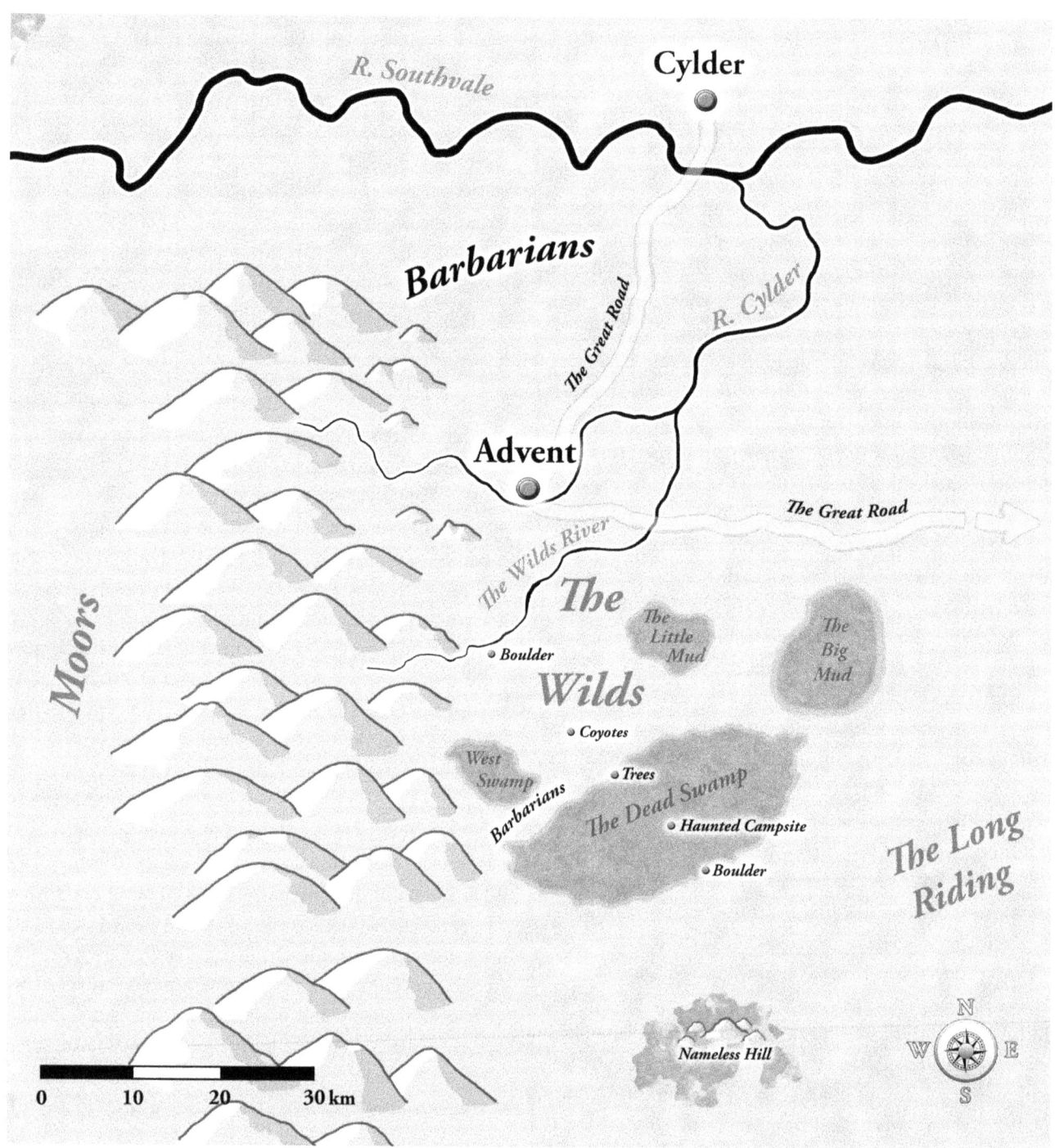

CYLDER, THE LONG RIDING, THE MOORS AND ENVIRONS

The History of Hessaret's Treasure

Hessaret's name is still infamous amongst the frontier folk. Most in Advent know him as a terrible villain of history. Some know him for the great love he shared with his loyal warrior-mate Bōdda, immortalised in an epic poem. The barbarians of the plains sing sagas of Hessaret's heroic exploits, inspiring the occasional young warrior to boast of being Hessaret incarnate, but such crowing leads nowhere, as the lesson of Hessaret's fall was well learned. Stories about Hessaret's fabled treasure hoard abound. After all, he pillaged the countryside for many years, and those heaps of loot must have gone somewhere... Legend says he hid his greatest treasure in the nearby frontier, but in a place so secret that when he died even his kin could not claim it.

Over the years, parties of bold (and foolhardy) adventurers have set out to find the trove, never to return again. Rumours say the ghosts of Hessaret and his barbarian horde roam the wild plains, killing anyone who seeks to rob him. Others are more pragmatic, saying the Wilds are filled with venomous beasts and monsters, and only a fool courts death in this way. Once a group of well-borne and well-equipped Adventines vowed they would find the hoard, or die trying! A month later the families mounted a search, hiring some skilful mercenaries to find their missing relatives. Neither the original party nor the mercenaries ever returned. Nowadays, anyone who talks of seeking Hessaret's treasure is ridiculed or beaten until they change their minds. Most people treat the stories of Hessaret's treasure as stories alone—fables to tempt the greedy and unwary.

But there is some truth to these fables. Hessaret's success was due largely to the mobility of his encampment. His most magnificent treasure was not suitably mobile, though, so it was hidden well. Its location, far from the circuit of campsites, was a secret shared only with a handful of trusted lieutenants—or so he believed. Unknown to Hessaret, on one occasion, a daring underling followed him to the trove, scrawling a map. The sneak never got the chance to exploit this knowledge, though.

On the fateful day of the Battle of Advent, this underling was amongst those left behind to mind the slaves at camp. When the main barbarian force had not returned for two days, the captives finally mustered the courage to rise up against their outnumbered masters and paid back years of mistreatment in a single bloody hour. From that carnage, the map was recovered by a former slave, who returned to The Vale to rebuild her life. In that distant land the map became a family heirloom. However, it remained an impotent curiosity, as she would not recount anything from the degradation that was her captivity, so upon her death the locations of the bandit encampments were lost. From parent to child, the map was handed down, but without a clear starting point a quest for the treasure seemed more and more hopeless to each generation.

Thus, when her great-great-grandson's grandson had inherited the map and his family fell on hard times, he decided that enough was enough and, in desperation, sold the chart for a handful of silver Founders. The buyer was the notorious bandit Karl Pig-Axe, who, after peddling it with no luck for several seasons, was glad to unload the trinket and its story on his associate Zarand in distant Advent, for double what he had paid.

As a resident of Advent, Zarand already knew well the legend of the Lost Hoard when he was offered the map, and he wagered that the item might be genuine. He promptly divided it in two for security, keeping one half on his person and hiding the other. Over the course of a year, his research revealed further bits of history, and recently he sent Arkannad into the Wilds to search for the landmark boulder near a river, as depicted on the map. When the scout identified such a rock, Zarand became convinced that he had placed the starting point for the map.

Two days ago, he announced this to his gang and they began to prepare for an expedition. Yesterday, Tobias decided to murder his boss for the map. Today, the adventure begins.

Tobias & Co

Tobias, Arkannad, Finiel, and Loram have been Zarand's loyal cohorts in all sorts of shady dealings, but the revelation about the treasure map has proved too tempting for Tobias, and the ambitious and unscrupulous rogue will eliminate his boss to steal it. Sensing trouble, Zarand has told Finiel (whom he likes best) about the second, hidden piece of the map, just in case anything should happen to him. She will recover the hidden piece before Tobias realises it exists.

Zarand's murder will sunder the gang, pitting Finiel and her devotee Loram against Tobias and his bodyguard Arkannad. These four rogues have very different personalities and motivations, all described in detail at the end of the scenario. How the adventurers fit into this picture will depend on whose story they believe, and their own personalities and motivations. It is envisioned (but not required) that the adventurers will be a stabilising influence to keep the antagonists working together towards their common goal of finding the hoard.

USING HESSARET'S TREASURE WITH BOOK OF QUESTS

Although this scenario is quite separate from the seven scenarios in *Book of Quests*, it can be easily slotted into that campaign in several ways.

First, it could act as a general introductory scenario that brings the characters together before they begin the *Book of Quests* campaign.

Second, it could form a chapter of *Book of Quests* that has nothing to do with the main campaign and acts as a diversion between events described in the book. References to Advent, Hessaret and the lost hoard might be found in any of the places described in *Book of Quests*, especially Cylder or Lurien. Alternatively, the characters might encounter Tobias, Finiel or others in their dealings with Lord Drystan, Karl PigAxe or others.

Finally, Hessaret's lost treasure might include a powerful artefact or weapon needed either by The Order of Truth or Jedakiah. The character might be sent to Advent by someone such as Lord Drystan to try to locate the hoard in order to strengthen the battle against the Sorcerer. Jedakiah would be likely to have his own agents in Advent - and possibly working with Tobias and the others. The scenario could then become a tense race to find the treasure involving Jedakiah's agents and the characters. If the agents are part of Tobias's group (or even the *entire* group) this could make for an interesting contest of wits, bluff and combat.

Exploring Advent

Advent nucleated around the watchtower about 160 years ago and has expanded in a roughly circular manner, to host 3000 or so people presently. Shrines, shops, and inns have become additional nuclei. Over time, families have grown, adding new dwellings and shops adjacent to their primary ones, and in places, these compounds have fused to form entire neighbourhoods. The gaps have been filled with tatty hovels that are the smallest step up from homelessness.

Many such shacks back up against the timber palisades that have marked the edge of town over the years. Both the original and second barriers remain, but sections have been removed for passages. The active palisade is quite strong and high (4 metres), with the bottom set in a 1.5-metre wall of mortared stone, and a gateway at each compass point. The latest generation of dwellings and shops has sprung up outside the wall and is not yet dense enough to fuse into neighbourhoods.

The finest buildings here are mortared stone, but most are wattle and daub; all have thatched roofs. While a few have second storeys, most are one floor and but a single room, perhaps with a loft for sleeping. Hovels are little more than thatch with a few supports, or even just piled branches. A few public wells have been dug for easy access to water. Fires are fuelled by wood or dung, and the air is full of the smell and occasionally heavy with smoke. The odours of animals and humans—and their wastes—are also strong, but are masked somewhat by those of cooking foods; street vendors are a common feature of Advent.

The streets can be viewed as narrow spaces where buildings have not yet encroached. Most are wide enough to conduct two carts abreast, but some alleys are as narrow as a man. All are packed earth, muddy in hard rain and dusty in the heat of summer. The layout is roughly concentric overall, but the irregular network of streets is more like a warren than a web; navigating it effectively requires the Streetwise skill. The only straight passage through town is the Great Road. A few avenues are wide enough to be squares, where pedlars can hawk their merchandise. The largest marketplace abuts the Great Road, of course, opposite the garrison.

Consistent with its origins, Advent has shrines to various deities, yet no proper temples. There are minor sites to honour the Founding Four pantheon, but proper worship requires a pilgrimage to Cylder. All the deities of The Realm are recognised, but the Renegade Gods of the barbarians are more frequent - especially to Renamos the Rising Storm. The people of Advent are, on the whole, a little less devout than residents of The Vale.

The town is dominated by trade and travellers, and there are many dozens of shopkeepers and pedlars dealing in raw materials and finished goods. All common and some rare items are available here; adventurer's gear like horses and tack, rope, torches, oil, candles, preserved food, tools, weapons, and some armour is easy to come by. Many residents—especially those attempting to sell something—are well practised at hospitality, but others are downright rude, and even prone to fight, if they think they can win.

There is an air of vitality in Advent, but with an edge of desperation. Many day labourers live in poverty, and below them still are beggars. Except in the worst weather, there are always people loitering, even late into the night. Some are criminals, and muggings are common. Adventurers who look dangerous or have bad reputations generally will not be accosted, but anyone else might be. The sense of always being watched is strong here and takes some getting used to.

It will not take long for strangers in Advent to be targeted by street urchins looking for a handout. Who can blame them? They certainly look pitiable… Their true nature is more complex, but at base they are children and they are needy. Adult townsfolk look coldly upon visitors who refuse to cough up a Penny or a crust of bread, whilst they look favourably upon those who are generous. Anyone foolish enough to harm one of these waifs, even by accident, provokes any nearby adults to hostility and possibly mob violence. The locals may not care enough to spare these children the ravages of penury, but they will not tolerate physical abuse—especially by strangers. All of the urchins in town know this and will play this card mercilessly as needed.

The current commander of the garrison, Captain Ulster, is a distant cousin of Lord Drystan of Senholm and is the most minor sort of nobility. He is the ultimate authority figure in Advent, but, as he sees it, policing the town is not his business—nor anyone else's. This is not The Vale. Justice is done by mob rule, with some influence from priests and community elders, in accordance with cultural norms plus local customs. If outraged citizens were to drag an accused criminal before the commander (which does happen occasionally), then he would be forced into action, at his own discretion and best judgement, but he does not take an active interest in the everyday affairs of the townsfolk. His soldiers do not patrol the town. If the adventurers object to the way they are being treated, then they must handle it themselves.

Characters from other cultures probably find the accents, manner of dress, and customs of Advent rather different from those of their homelands and therefore quite interesting, yet fatiguing. Even villagers from the region

URCHINS, URCHINS EVERYWHERE!

These children are perhaps the most obvious sign of poverty in Advent, and the place seems to be crawling with them. Finiel knows and employs most of them, here and there. They spy and run errands for her, and she pays merchants around town to feed and clothe them (albeit at the level of bare subsistence). This is a business arrangement; Finiel uses these guttersnipes like she uses everyone else, though she does empathise with them, having grown up that way herself. They like her and appreciate the attention, and want to please her by following her orders.

A typical urchin is five to ten years old, underfed, unwashed, barefoot, and clothed in rags. Those who are not orphans nonetheless have parents who cannot (or do not) provide for them. Girls and boys are met with about equal frequency. Their demeanour and behaviour run the full gamut, from abject begging to playful name-calling, from genuine innocence to calculated pocket-picking. The characters will encounter urchins several times around town, and the Games Master is encouraged to play these meetings to the hilt, for pathetic or comic value.

These ragamuffins are usually met in sizeable groups and are not characterised individually, being most easily treated as Rabble (MYTHRAS, page 111) with a mere 2 Hit Points each. Their most interesting skills are Acting, Athletics, Deceit, Evade, Perception, Sleight, Stealth, Streetwise, and Unarmed (most often used to Grapple), at the 30–40% level generally. These urchins carry no weapons and almost never engage in combat, though they might harass a character by pushing, grabbing, and hanging on, or throwing garbage or rocks. One child grabbing at the legs is a nuisance, but five are a real obstacle. Most have a surprisingly sophisticated repertoire of group tactics, and an adventurer may find that whilst dealing with a few on the left, his purse has been lightened by others from the right.

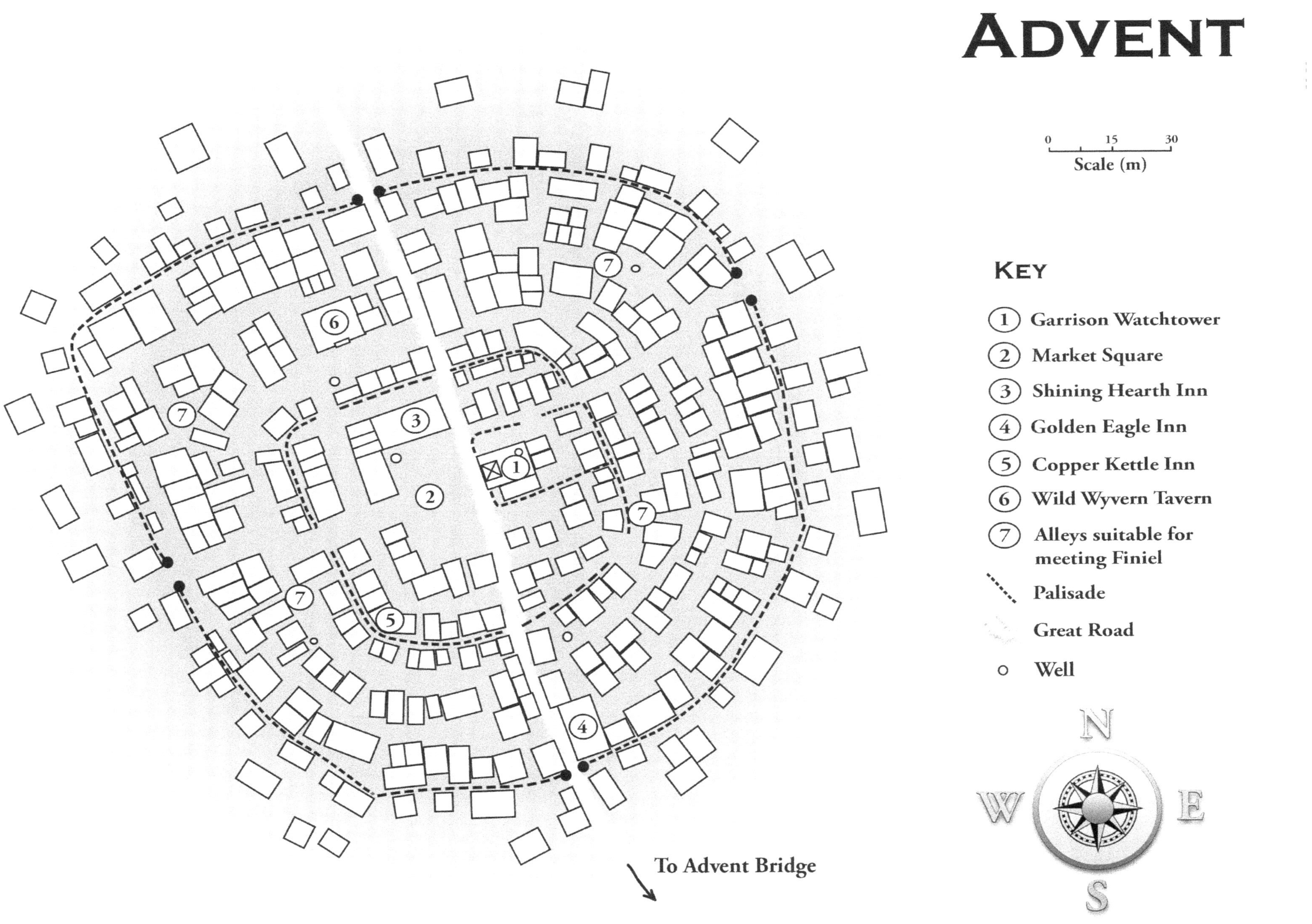

ADVENT

Scale (m)
0 — 15 — 30

KEY

1. Garrison Watchtower
2. Market Square
3. Shining Hearth Inn
4. Golden Eagle Inn
5. Copper Kettle Inn
6. Wild Wyvern Tavern
7. Alleys suitable for meeting Finiel
- - - Palisade
─── Great Road
○ Well

To Advent Bridge

may be overwhelmed by the sights, sounds, and smells of town life. By the end of the day, they should be well ready for a pint and a bed.

There are a handful of inns about town, easily found, but they all claim to be full. The Shining Hearth, the Golden Eagle, the Copper Kettle—at place after place, the proprietor declares that there are no rooms left at all. There simply are not that many beds in town, so they are usually close to sold out during the seasons when merchants are active—first come, first served. Faced with sleeping in the street, the characters finally learn about the Wild Wyvern Tavern, a rowdy establishment run by a man called Piggins. "You might go there for a drink and a song, or a fight, but certainly not to stay," warns a townsperson. Well, how bad could it be, really...and what choice do they have? A chilly fog is descending as clouds gather. They should at least check out the place.

Mayhem at the Wild Wyvern

Outside the main entrance, the characters are again accosted by urchins (six or eight, or as many as the Games Master prefers, and not necessarily the same ones as were met earlier) who beg for food and money. They insert themselves between the strangers and the door to prolong their entreaties, but will not continue inside when the adventurers push through. It should strike the characters that even homeless children should not be out in the street so late, never mind hanging about the seediest establishment in town. (These wayward youths are not here by chance, in fact.)

The Wild Wyvern tavern is as dodgy as the adventurers were warned to expect...but it is warm and dry, if somewhat rank. At this hour, the place boasts an assortment of 15 or so drinkers, but is not truly crowded. A handful of them surround two of their friends, who are locked in a dogged bout of arm wrestling. At another table, a trio rolls dice, alternately cursing and cheering their luck. The background volume of chatter is considerable. The great room is dimly lit and smells of spilled beer, wood smoke, sweat, and urine. A low but steady fire burns without cheer in a large stone hearth. A Perception check reveals a rat scurrying along the base of the far wall; another reveals a dark, heavy curtain near the door to the kitchen. Any character who tries to peek behind the curtain is rebuffed by a hard look from a scary wild man (Arkannad), who growls and yanks the barrier back in place.

Also of note is a tremendous young man standing near the hearth, arms folded. This is Loram the Large. He has brown eyes and long brown hair and beard, with a ruddy face drawn down in a scowl. Though dressed as a commoner, without armour, he carries himself like a warrior. He watches the tavern's guests with an intent, practised gaze. He is clearly an enforcer, there to keep unruly customers in check.

Piggins, the proprietor, a brusque and slovenly creature, greets the characters tersely and waves them to one of the large tables towards the back of the room. He takes their orders for simple food and drink, and confirms that there are lodgings available. "Sure, there's always rooms here, if ye want 'em."

Soon another patron enters the bar, a thin middle-aged man with a carefree, almost regal, bearing. He casts his eyes about and crosses the room to clap Loram on the shoulder. They exchange quiet words, and the newcomer turns to eye the adventurers. With an approving glance and a smile, he doffs his fashionable hat and approaches their table. "Welcome! I have not seen you here before. My name is Zarand. May I join you?" He attempts the customary pleasantries, to learn their names, origins, and intent. Zarand reveals that he is a native Adventine (which is the truth) and a merchant (which is a lie). He is vague about the details of his business ("acquisitions and fulfilment") and deftly shifts the subject. "Are you looking for work? You seem...capable. I can always use more quick hands and strong backs. ... Stay awhile. I have a meeting now, but I'll come back to you later, and we can discuss your terms. Meanwhile, have a drink on me." He lays the appropriate number of silver Founders on the table and disappears behind the curtain by the bar. The characters have a chance to debate Zarand's actual profession and what their own terms of employment might be.

It is not long before a server arrives with food and grog. While munching their uninspired victuals, and perhaps questioning their decision not to sleep outside, at least one of the adventurers is sure to hear a distant ruckus coming from a back room—from behind the curtain, in fact. Every character needs to make a Hard Perception roll to take in the details of what happens next, for the action is rapid and the room is dim and noisy. Failure yields only a general impression, and a fumble means the character sneezed or had her head turned, but a critical success means any question about the event may be asked of the Games Master, now or later.

The Wild Wyvern Tavern

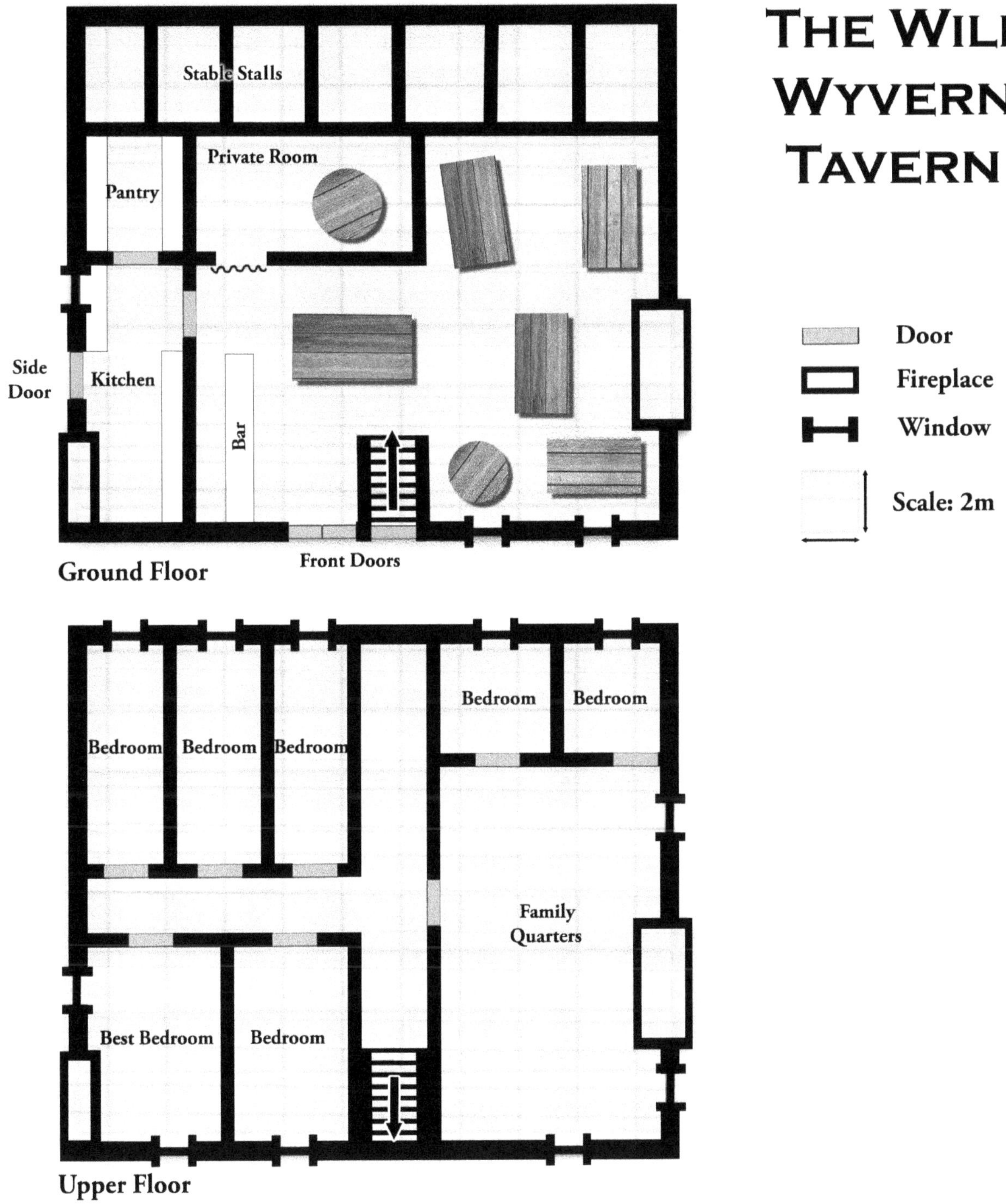

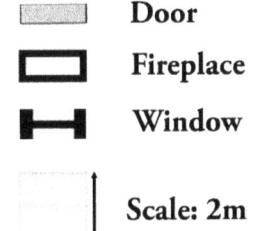

Stable Stalls
Private Room
Pantry
Side Door
Kitchen
Bar
Front Doors
Ground Floor
Door
Fireplace
Window
Scale: 2m
Bedroom
Bedroom
Bedroom
Bedroom
Bedroom
Family Quarters
Best Bedroom
Bedroom
Upper Floor

There is a crash of falling furniture from behind the curtain and a lithe woman dashes out, gracefully dodging chairs and a serving wench. This is Finiel. Her clothes are fashionable but a bit worn. Her long, light-brown hair streams behind her as she pelts out the door into the night. She must be very coordinated to move like that. Everyday townies do not possess such skill....

Due to surprise, Finiel will be out of the tavern before any character can do more than stand up, and most will not even manage that. What comes next should be handled by Initiative in combat rounds.

Loram the Large hesitates for just a moment, then moves to pursue Finiel; the adventurers could try to stop him or follow along. They might easily mistake that Loram is chasing Finiel to catch her and perhaps do her some harm, which could affect their decision to pursue or ignore either one. Loram doesn't think, he acts, and charges through contact (MYTHRAS, page 102), overturning tables, chairs, and patrons as needed, to leave and follow his comrade.

Characters chasing Finiel out in the streets are most unlikely to keep up, as she is athletic and knows this town well. She also has laid a trap for would-be pursuers: Those urchins whom the adventurers met on the way into the tavern are still outside, and now pounce upon them with real vigour, grabbing limbs or clothing to distract, slow, or even trip the strangers chasing their mistress. They will retreat into the mist if attacked, or when their mission to interfere seems completed,

Trying to catch Finiel is further hindered by the foggy bad weather that has driven the adventurers to the tavern in the first place. Even Loram will probably lose them in this mess. He does not want to fight at this time, but, of course, he will, if attacked—or if he thinks it will aid his partner's escape. His Brawn and Athletics serve him well in using impromptu weapons. If somehow Loram is captured or convinced not to flee, he actually cooperates a little. An Insight check leads him to identify himself and the other members of his gang, but then clam up. "You need to talk to Finiel."

Note that even if the characters have refused to seek out the Wild Wyvern and instead are lounging outside in the weather, Finiel and then Loram will dash by them at this stage, and children will still pop up to harry them.

So, what exactly has happened at the Wild Wyvern? Any character not leaving the premises, or returning promptly, may jostle through the crowd and poke a head behind the curtain, only to find the dangerous-looking, smelly barbarian occupying the doorway. A voice from within tells the savage to stand aside; fearful townies remain at a distance, but a nosy adventurer will not be barred.

Beyond the curtain is a private room with a medium round table and seating for four. Two chairs are overturned and the dinner on the table is in disarray, a fallen cup of wine dripping its last onto the floor. A well-dressed man with dark hair (Tobias) rises from one knee to address the character, quietly but earnestly. "Are you a healer? Can you help my friend? He's not breathing." He gestures behind the table, where the characters can see the upper body of another man: Zarand, who greeted them pleasantly not long ago. Even if someone here does know Healing, there's really nothing to be done: By this time, the man is plainly dead.

The corpse is unwounded, but its lips and tongue are slightly discoloured. Anyone with Healing can see that Zarand seems to have been poisoned. There are mushrooms on his plate but, success with Lore (Fungi, Poisons, or Cooking), or with Locale at Hard grade, reveals that all of the mushrooms in his dinner appear to be harmless. A Formidable Perception roll reveals that the clothing of the deceased lies in an unnatural way, following a fall. It looks as if he has been searched.

Once any efforts to revive Zarand have concluded and the apparent cause of death has been announced, the remaining onlookers murmur, gasp, and disperse. Piggins, trailed by the serving wench, barges in to gawk and exclaim, "I can't be having this in my place! It's not right, not clean! Who's gonna handle this, now?" Tobias presses a coin into his hand and says, "Get someone to bring him to an empty room, quickly and quietly—and throw out the rest of that slop you served him, before someone else dies. I'll have him out before dawn." Turning to the characters, he asks, "Where did she go?"

Whether or not they respond honestly, or at all, Tobias will put his hand on Arkannad's shoulder and firmly instructs, "Find her." The barbarian stalks off without a word.

The adventurers surely have questions. At this stage, check Tobias's Deceit versus each listener's Insight to see how well his story goes over. What he says is basically true; the only question is whether a listener senses that he is holding something back.

Tobias introduces himself and names all the other gang members as "business partners". ("What business? Never mind...this and that...you know.") The characters may mention that Zarand had offered them employment, to which Tobias replies knowingly, "Makes sense. You look like you can handle yourselves and Zarand is…was always looking for new talent." According to Tobias, Zarand had called a meeting of the gang; Loram stayed out in the main room because he sometimes works for Piggins and was scheduled for that night. After a few bites of food, Zarand started gagging and turning pale, then hit the floor. Tobias and Arkannad tried to help, but Finiel just leaped up and ran out. "I don't know why. All I know is that my old friend lies cold and you tell me it was poison. A hasty person might suppose the worst. Indeed, just yesterday Zarand was worried…well, never mind that, now. If I catch up to Finiel, you can be sure I'll get some answers. Come to think of it, maybe you could help with that. It would be worth your while. How about a Royal to retrieve her?" A gold piece should strike the characters as rather a lot for such a modest task. He really must want to find this partner of his.

Whether or not they agree to help him, Tobias does not detain the adventurers; he is busy enough for now, having to arrange for Zarand's final repose. If they agree to help find Finiel, he thanks them and says not to worry about meeting up again. "We'll find you. There's nothing that goes on in Advent that we don't hear about." He departs the tavern, even if the characters decide to stay. They still have no place else to sleep indoors, yet now are confronted not only with vermin, but also a corpse in the next room. A sleepless night should give them ample opportunity to discuss clues and impressions, at least.

From the Wild Wyvern, Tobias quickly heads across town to ransack Zarand's abode, only to find that what he seeks is gone. Cursing Finiel and her quick feet, he steals back to his own chambers to study the half of the treasure map that he found on Zarand's person and ponder his next move. Any character following Tobias out of the tavern needs to pit his Stealth versus Tobias' Perception, perhaps modified for the conditions outdoors; if Tobias discovers that he is being tailed, he uses his undoubtedly superior Streetwise skill to shake any pursuers. He will not head for Zarand's home or his own until he is sure that he is no longer being followed.

It is unlikely that an adventurer will catch Tobias in the act of tearing up the apartment (which they may not even realise is Zarand's), but even if one did, little could be concluded from this strange observation. In any case, if an adventurer happens to find her way to Zarand's place, an Easy Insight roll reveals that someone was desperately looking for something. Bedclothes, furniture, apparel, trinkets—everything is strewn on the floor or dishevelled.

A Plea for Help

Whether or not the adventurers go looking for Finiel, she finds them. Doubtless, they want to quit their squalid lodgings early the next morning, at least to get some air and a little decent food. Before long, they are trailed in the busy street by a stooped crone in a tattered shawl, who nudges the one closest to the alley on the right and whispers, "Psst! Don't look! Come into the shadows here. I need your help. Please!" If ignored, the old woman displays sudden vigour in attempting to pull her mark into the alley. Even if she fails, at least she gets his attention. "I'm not joking here. They'll kill me!"

Finiel has orchestrated this encounter carefully, and if the adventurers try to seize her, she simply escapes down the partially blocked alley (read on). If instead they opt to talk, she tells her version of the story to Influence them. It is not all lies: She truly (and correctly) believes that Tobias killed Zarand for the map and would treat her likewise. She wants the protection of the adventurers, as well as the leverage they present for realising her plans. All of this lends credence to her words, even as she tries to conceal her other motivations.

Presently, Finiel wants three things: the treasure, defence against Tobias and Arkannad, and revenge for Zarand's murder. One way to attain all three is to keep Tobias close, so that she can use him and his half of the map to get the hoard, keep an eye on him to avoid a sneak attack, and get him alone out in the wilderness for her own surprise attack. After she joined back up with Loram, they talked late into last night, and she realised that the strangers he described might be just the tools for her job. The locals are too familiar with Tobias and his bodyguard to tangle with them, but perhaps these outsiders might be convinced to assist and even mediate.

An adventurer trying to follow Finiel down the alley finds it blocked by a well-placed cart that she has expertly surmounted. Approaching the cart, the character is mobbed (yet again) by pesky urchins making quite a bit of noise and drawing possibly unwanted attention. From the far side of the cart, the same huge, bearded man from the tavern last night (Loram) points at them ominously, then retreats. By the time a character has made it to the crowded street beyond, both Finiel and Loram are gone.

If the characters are gullible enough to agree so soon to help Finiel, she thanks them profusely but still leaves them at this stage, just not so dramatically.

> ### FINIEL ACTS DESPERATE
>
> The following are selections of what Finiel might say. Adjust as needed.
>
> *You were at the Wild Wyvern last night. You know what happened to Zarand, then?*
>
> *Ate a bad mushroom, my arse! Oh, Zarand was poisoned, all right, but it wasn't bad food. That traitor Tobias did it, curse him...and I'm next. If he would do that to the boss, then there's no telling what he'd do to me. I need protection.*
>
> *Why? Because the boss had something Tobias wants, and if that rat didn't find it he'll probably think I have it and come after me.*
>
> *I should explain. The dead fellow you saw was Zarand. He was our boss, the four of us: me, Loram, that snake Tobias, and his barbarian Arkannad. Watch out for him, too. Arkannad's as weird as the day is long—no knowing what he'll say or do next. He listens to Tobias, though.*
>
> *Anyway, we do all sorts of work: buying, selling, finding things, finding people, getting information...you understand. There have been others, come and gone, but it was always the four of us, and then lately the five of us, with Arkannad. We were a good team, but now, this. I can't believe it. Zarand's just...gone. He was like a father to me!*
>
> *What drove Tobias to murder? What difference does it make?! What matters is he did it, which means he'll stop at nothing. I'm not safe! I spent last night hiding in a haystack, for pity's sake. Are you going to help me, or what? I can pay.*
>
> *I cannot stay. I have lingered too long already! He has eyes everywhere. Someone will fetch you later, so that we may come to an arrangement.*

A PROPOSITION

The adventurers have a few hours to debate whether they should help Finiel or turn her in to Tobias. That afternoon, however, Tobias finds them, whether it be in the marketplace, the tavern, or an alley. He expects a response to his offer to hunt Finiel, unless the characters have already agreed to that, in which case he expects a report. He is alone; Arkannad seems to be off on the hunt. In truth, the barbarian watches the scene from concealment, a short run away, just in case things should somehow go wrong for Tobias.

Whether or not the adventurers tell Tobias the truth is up to them. If they probe for the reason Finiel might have had to poison Zarand, Tobias is distrusting; he is keenly aware that the characters may have already discussed the situation with Finiel. If they simply tell him all, or fail to deceive him, then any doubts are gone. Sensing this, he takes the opportunity to be (mostly) honest with them—and to manipulate them to be on his side, using money, promises of power, etc. Tobias appears generous, weaving a future to appeal to the characters' aspirations.

In contrast to Finiel, Tobias becomes calmer and more nonchalant as he chats with the adventurers. He is the epitome of a confidence man. When it comes time to discuss the hoard, though, he has to check his Passion for wealth against his Willpower to conceal his lust from listeners. (Failure just augments his attempt to Influence the characters, really.)

STRIKING A DEAL

Assuming the adventurers don't drop the whole affair and leave town, they have a few options:

- Find Finiel and convince her to accept Tobias's proposition. Maybe she even has a counter-offer.
- Find Finiel, overpower her, and bring her to Tobias. This probably means fighting not just her but Loram as well, which could easily leave a character crippled or dead and no closer to the treasure. To improve their chances, they could first try to neutralise Loram in isolation, but even that seems dangerous. Perhaps it is quaint to consider, but some characters

TOBIAS'S PITCH

The following are selections of what Tobias might say. Adjust as needed.

Why kill Zarand? An excellent question. It kept me up most of the night. I'd like to ask Finiel myself. I suppose it comes down to avarice, my friends—simple, ugly greed. I went by Zarand's early this morning to get him some burial clothes, only to find the place ransacked. She must have been there.

Searching for what? Well, the boss had some wealth tucked away, to be sure, but from the look of things she must have sought something in particular, something especially valuable.

Mm? Yes, "what" indeed. I have come to the conclusion that it must have been...well, it's private, really...all right, all right, there's no way around it. You're in this up to your eyes already. It's just an old scrap of paper, but if the boss was right, it's worth a fortune. It's a map—a treasure map.

Some time ago Zarand got his hands on this old, old map. A guy he knew from across the river sold it to him, said it used to be some kind of family heirloom to a fellow whose great-great-somebody had been with a villain named Hessaret. A barbarian hero, the "Black Scourge of the Frontier"; ever heard of him? He's legend around here. Zarand realised that if this heirloom story turned out to be true, we could all get rich—rich as kings.

Long before the time of our grandfathers, this Hessaret used to pillage the whole countryside, for years and years. They never could catch him and his bandits...well, until they finally did. He got greedy and tried to take Advent itself, but the king's soldiers were lying in wait for him, and that was that. But nobody ever found his hoard. Think about it: years of stealing from everyone around—villagers, merchants, soldiers—piles and piles of gold and jewels, yet nobody knows where it all went! So, over time, Zarand dug around for tales and lore and slowly, bit by bit, became sure that this map of his was the real thing. He told us, what, a couple of days ago? Seems a lot longer, somehow.

We started settling our business and preparing for an expedition, but then last night...you saw. Finiel must have got it in her head to steal the map and poison Zarand—probably all of us, for that matter. I hadn't even taken a bite of my dinner yet and I wasn't about to try it afterwards.

I think that wretch got a little less than she bargained for, though. Serves her right. See, the boss was clever: He tore that map in two and hid the pieces separately. I know, because the day before yesterday he gave me the other half. He said he suspected treachery, but when I asked what he meant by that, he just shook his head and told me to stay wary and keep that piece of the map safe. Never you mind where I put it; that's my safety. If anything happens to me, the treasure is lost.

So, it appears we have a bit of a situation here. Half a treasure map is useless by itself, but what to do? I can't trust Finiel, not after what she did to Zarand. But it seems to me there is something she did not count on: you. If you can persuade her to parley with me to work out a deal, then we may yet solve this conundrum.

Me, sell my half? You're joking. There's not enough gold in the whole frontier. Finiel probably knows that, too, come to think of it. And before you think about trying to take the map from me, let's just save us all the inconvenience. I don't want to fight you, but I will, and I doubt it would go well for either us. Even if you won, I would never break under torture. Neither would Finiel, I suspect. She's a tough little thief.

No, I suppose instead we'll all end up working together, so I'll tell you what: I'll hire you to watch my back, and Arkannad's, and be the go-between. If Finiel agrees, we all go get the treasure together and split it three ways: one part for Arkannad and me, one part for Finiel and Loram, and a third for you.

On the other hand, considering how things went for poor Zarand, I have to say that if you turn up here with the map in hand, and no one ever hears from Finiel again, I won't ask any questions. Then we could split the hoard just two ways. That's up to you.

Well, what do you say? Do you want to be rich? It's the chance of a lifetime. Go, now. Think about it. Meet me at the Wild Wyvern tonight—preferably with Finiel, or her half of the map.

who would pretend to be decent members of society might actually object to this sort of brutality on principles. Anyhow, so much bloodshed in the days following the arrival of the adventurers could bring the soldiery down on them.

- Find Finiel, overpower her, and steal her part of the map. Barring fanciful helpings of stealth and luck, this too means fighting her and Loram. She is as tricky as Tobias and has already hidden her part, so the characters would come away empty-handed anyway. Then they would have to resort to torture, which Tobias has warned them might not even work.
- Attack Tobias on the spot, while he is alone, and force him to give up his part of the map. Again, if this even were to work, it would eventually require torture—but it probably would not work, because Arkannad is lurking and watching, ready to help Tobias. Attacking could spell quick doom for the characters.

Discussion and roleplaying should lead the group to the first option; the remainder of the scenario is written with this in mind. If they choose a more violent approach, then they may never make it out of Advent alive, considering the threat posed by either faction of gangsters and the frontier justice they would receive from the locals.

As the shadows grow long, two waifs, apparently brother and sister, approach the characters with a message: "Quick-feet said to bring you to her. Follow us!" The children swiftly lead them on a labyrinthine path to the outer palisade, then out of town to the northeast on the main road. "Keep going for about a league. Look for the big man at the old elm tree on the right."

These simple and accurate directions do in fact lead to Loram, who whistles low from the gathering darkness beneath the massive elm. Now armoured and bearing his mighty hammer, he looks every bit the warrior that the characters suspected. "Were you followed? No. Good. Come."

About 100 metres into light woods Loram whistles again, and they step down into a small clearing with a campfire and two lean-tos. Finiel stands dappled in firelight, resplendent in her adventuring gear. In marked contrast to her earlier performance, she now seems confident and collected—haughty, even. "We meet again. So, what's your price to help us out?"

The details of the ensuing conversation hinge on whether the characters reveal that they know about the map. If they intend to persuade her to follow Tobias's plan, Loram observes attentively but silently.

During the conversation, Finiel realises (but does not announce) that the best way to get a clear shot at her enemy—away from civilisation and without being hunted down by these outsiders—is by following his own plan. She is not the type to truck in murder for hire; in any case, she cannot afford to hire the characters to kill Tobias (and dares not, presently, since he has surely hidden his part of the map). Knowing full well that Tobias may have already made a similar offer for killing her, she boldly quizzes the characters to gauge their reactions. Even if they are cool or confirm her suspicion, she will not be deterred. Finiel is

FINIEL'S STORY

That son of a jackal! Is that what he told you? Lies! Yes, we were all at supper that night, but as soon as Zarand started looking funny and grabbing his throat, Tobias got right up close to him, as if to help—but it was really just to pick him over for the map. I wish I could have seen his face when he found only half of it...but, believe me, I didn't stick around long enough.

You see, earlier in the day the boss had taken me aside and given me the other half, because he was afraid of—well, exactly what happened! He said he knew he could count on me and that if anything went wrong he wanted me to have the treasure. He didn't trust Tobias, but decided to stay cool and keep him close to keep an eye on him. That was a big mistake. Oh, I just know Tobias did him in. I know it in my bones! Zarand was good to me and he deserved better. Tobias had better not show me his back.

Prove it? You want to see my part of the map? Hah! Do I look stupid? If anything happens to me, it'll never be found. Even Loram here doesn't know where I stashed it.

Now, a man who kills his own boss for a treasure map doesn't hesitate to hire strangers to kill his comrades for same. Surely you're too smart to go down that road, though. Remember what I said: anything happens to me and the map is lost. Besides, the last guy that tried to hurt me can only eat soup now. Loram's hammer doesn't miss.

tough and a bit of a gambler, and she does have Loram to back her up. She just wants to get a sense of these strangers.

In the end, Finiel admits that Tobias' plan seems the best resolution they are likely to achieve, and she and Loram agree to join in. "We'll meet you all at Advent Bridge, at noon tomorrow. Now, go tell that weasel the good news. We have preparations to make."

If the characters return to the hideout for any reason, they find it abandoned. Finiel is too clever to be caught so easily.

Tobias is very pleased (and a little surprised) by the news and buys the characters drinks late into the night. He agrees to meet them at the bridge as suggested. He also promises to make all survivors his partners upon return to Advent and tries to hire them to watch his back on the expedition. "If I make it back to Advent unharmed by either of those two, I'll give every one of you an extra bag of gold." What exactly he means by that is up for discussion, though nit-picking such a generous offer might come off as rather gauche. If this hoard is half as grand as it sounds, there will be plenty of extra wealth for loyal supporters. Tobias, meanwhile, is willing to promise the adventurers anything that sounds remotely plausible—and just as willing to renege later.

THE COMPANY FORMS

The adventurers have the next morning to plan how best to handle the reunion of the gang's factions, and to purchase any last-minute gear, such as food, rope, torches, arrows, kits for First Aid or Healing, or beasts of burden.

The morning fog burns off as the sun climbs in the sky. To get to Advent Bridge, one just follows the Great Road south out of town; characters who came from the south already know this. Tobias and Arkannad are waiting for them. Tobias rides a horse, but Arkannad walks. Both now bear armour and weapons, which the characters have not yet seen; Arkannad looks wilder than ever in his bear skin. Finally, Finiel and Loram arrive, also armoured and ready. Loram leads a couple of pack mules he says he purchased that morning.

This meeting is a chance for chit chat and roleplaying, and for the adventurers to observe the group dynamic of the four former colleagues. The tension is palpable and the newcomers may feel the need to intervene to forestall violence. For example, when Tobias offers a skin of wine to toast the company's good fortune, Finiel and Loram refuse it with hard looks. Whether the others partake is up to them.

BONDING THROUGH COMMUNICATION

This and several other key spots in the story, such as while travelling or resting around a campfire, are opportunities for an adventurer to learn more about the Non-Player Characters' personalities, motivations, and behaviours. Insight is a very useful skill to this end, as is Acting, Deceit, or even Seduction. A character may be surprised to find that he actually has something in common with one of these scoundrels due to similar upbringing or other experiences. This sort of personal information and rapport is vital to avoiding surprises—especially at the climax of the scenario. Bonding now could later lead to taking one side of a conflict instead of another, and could significantly affect how the characters come out of the scenario.

# Into the Wilds

At an appropriate point (when making camp being the most likely, but it may also be while travelling) from a hidden flap on his horse's saddle, Tobias produces the first piece of the map (see opposite). It depicts the trail to the hoard beginning at a strange landmark with a hole in the middle by the side of a river, then proceeding to a spot marked by two trees at the edge of some threatening terrain. Arkannad has scouted out the landmark, a boulder on a southern spur of the River Cylder, and supposes that the strange terrain on the map must be the Dead Swamp in the Wilds southeast of Advent. The boulder marks one of Hessaret's many campsites: the one from which he was followed to his hoard by the map's maker. Locating this landmark enabled Zarand to solve the puzzle, without Arkannad even realising its significance.

The Wilds is wet short-grass prairie, with some marshy spots that are inconvenient but not dangerous, yet other spots of stony soil. Peoples in generations past tried to tame this land, but failed; there are scattered signs of their attempts. The soil is uneven and difficult to plough. Large mounds of broken rocks, as well as some huge boulders, protrude in frequent ridges and bumps. The wind picks up from time to time, and it tends to be unpleasantly cool and humid at night. Mist clings to the ground most nights and mornings. Infrequent stands of gnarled trees grow here and there. There is some water but most is foetid, so spending a long time here could be problematic. Game birds and small mammals abound; they eat wild berries, which adventurers could discover as well. Explorers still out at dusk can hear coyotes yelping in the distance.

Tobias has a decent Locale score, but that will not help in finding a good path here. Arkannad knows Navigation (Open Country) and has travelled some of the Wilds, including this stretch, and thus, is the natural leader for this part of the journey. If another character insists on taking the lead, Arkannad will defer, at Tobias's direction, but he and Tobias then stay right behind the leader. If at any stage the pathfinder gets the party lost or anything related to travelling goes wrong, then the leader is plagued with second-guessing, bickering, and accusations, mostly by Arkannad.

From the far side of Advent Bridge, the group leaves the road and heads south for about two hours to the rivulet they need to follow. Along the way they pass a few fieldstone foundations, the ruins of old farmhouses, but these contain nothing of interest. The cool, clear Wilds River

TOBIAS'S PORTION OF THE MAP

A NOTE ABOUT WEATHER

This scenario is set during a season with good weather, reasonable temperatures, and otherwise hospitable conditions. However, the Games Master could impose precipitation, harsh temperatures, or winds to challenge the company. Any of these adverse conditions shifts many skill rolls to one grade harder and prolongs travel. Strong winds make ascending Nameless Hill even more dangerous.

sparkles in the sun, and tracking it southwest back towards its source in the mountains is quite pleasant. After three hours of this, however, feet have begun to ache and no amount of pretty scenery can fix that. Fortunately, Arkannad points out that their first landmark, the unusual boulder Zarand had him scout, is just ahead.

On the far bank of the river stands a mighty grey-pink rock, fully 5 metres high and 3 metres across—roughly like a giant potato standing on end. This sandstone monolith has a remarkable hole bored smoothly through its middle. Probably none of the characters has ever seen anything like this oddity. From their point of view, it should strike them as a sort of window on the south. With the afternoon sun to warm them, this is an ideal spot to pause for a meal, soak in the river, water the horses, and strike up a conversation.

Fording the rivulet here is simple enough, and the party heads southwest across a rougher section of the prairie. The rest of the day will be spent here There are no signs of settlers on this side of the river. Check for fatigue as needed. Any mounted character, such as Tobias, needs to make one Ride roll: failure means the mount stumbles for 1d4 damage to a leg and −25% from base movement, while a fumble means this plus the rider being thrown for damage as if falling 2 metres. Check Navigation once: failure leads to an hour of wasted time, a fumble costs 1d2+1 hours, but a critical success puts them an hour ahead. The characters are not on a schedule, but the Games Master should keep track of any lost time because it could strongly affect where they stop at the end of the next day in the Dead Swamp.

As the sun sets, the next landmark on the map is not yet in sight, so the party stops at a place of their choice to make camp for the night. When the busywork is done and supper consumed, the adventurers have another natural opportunity at the fireside to sing, tell stories, or brag about past exploits.

They might demonstrate their talents using Influence, Deceit, Lore, Combat Styles, Athletics, or Acrobatics; the Games Master should encourage players to be creative. No matter what else may transpire, Loram challenges the largest of the newcomers to a wrestling match. Arkannad watches with interest but silently, then scoffs at the winner, prompting his own match. There is much to be learned from such tests of skill.

Even if nobody else does, Tobias eventually tires of these displays and calls the group to order. "Could we please be done with this? There's more ground to cover tomorrow and I could use some sleep."

COYOTE TROUBLE

Considering the intense distrust, each faction keeps its own watch. The adventurers may opt out, but that seems unwise amongst these scoundrels. As the first watch gets settled and the others bed down, howls and yips are heard from far away. Arkannad is unconcerned. "Those are coyotes, not wolves. They don't attack people or big animals. Go to sleep."

Coyotes are master scavengers, though, and investigate any strange smell. About an hour later, this particular pack cautiously approaches the explorers' camp. Arkannad was right: They will not attack the characters or their beasts—but they will attempt to steal any food that has not been secured. The mules or horses will probably have the first chance to notice their approach; check Perception for these animals, and then for people on watch, versus Stealth for the coyotes, who approach from downwind. A horse's sense of smell is not impeded by darkness, but a human's sight is. A horse or mule noticing a coyote will be visibly perturbed, but will not attempt to bolt.

If the coyotes get into position before a character notices, roll Athletics for each; success means provisions have been grabbed, and on its next turn, the beast will sprint off into the night with its spoils. An attacked coyote does not fight back but retreats at top speed, unless it has been trapped, grabbed, or wounded to immobility.

This nonlethal encounter is meant to make the adventurers' lives harder without ending them. Without their rations, they need to hunt (Perception or Track, followed by Stealth and Combat Style) or gather (Survival) something to eat the following day. This could take hours, and failure is sure to set people griping. On the other hand, it is a chance to bond with their companions and success earns goodwill.

Starvation is not yet a concern, but it is also not out of mind. There will be later opportunities to hunt or gather. Perhaps, it is time to start being nicer to Arkannad, with his good Survival training and all. At least the party still has water (for now).

BARBARIANS ON PATROL

Finally resuming their trek, the adventurers continue across the prairie for a few hours, until they come upon a landmark that is not on their map. On a small rise, they see three spears planted in the ground. A human skull tops each spear, the point punched through its crown. Fist-sized rocks are piled around the bases of the spears in some sort of ritual pattern.

Arkannad is nonchalant about this horrid discovery. "Hmph. Must be some tribe's territory. This is a warning. We should arm ourselves." This is good advice, for half an hour later the company is assaulted. An Easy Perception roll versus the Stealth of the assailants thwarts the surprise.

A group of young warriors from the Kamtot clan has set this ambush, having picked up the company's trail near the marker and raced ahead out of sight to this prime spot. They are eager to prove their manhood by repelling deadly invaders (or at least that is how they have built up their chore in their minds). They are looking for trouble and will not hesitate to attack at the right moment, flinging their javelins from high ground, and then waiting with axes ready for opponents to rush up at them.

The Kamtots are wild and brave and use deadly force, but flee if they sustain worse than Minor Wounds. Their job is to kill, capture, or drive off interlopers, and failing that to retreat and warn the clan of a significant threat. Fighting to the death would not only be foolish but also would jeopardise the safety of the entire tribe, and they understand this well, despite their youthful recklessness.

Each has a horse, which has been left out of sight nearby; a quick and definitive escape should be easy.

This is another nonlethal encounter (though riskier than the last) to foster camaraderie by fighting side by side, and to observe each other's skills. The Games Master should set the size of the patrol to be at least two fewer than the number in the company; the barbarians need to be significantly outnumbered or they might not flee.

A character succeeding at Insight notices that Loram leaps in to defend Finiel, even though she seems not to need it. Tobias needs more help than she does. Come to think of it, Loram likewise overreacted when the coyotes came...and he carries some of Finiel's gear for her...and he always serves her first at meals. If it has not crossed the character's mind before, it now occurs to him that Loram is sweet on Finiel and may not be fully rational when it comes to dealing with her.

If any of the barbarians is unable to flee yet still alive, the party must decide what to do with them. Finiel, Tobias, and Arkannad seem to have no qualms about killing barbarians and do not want to be bothered with prisoners. Loram, however, is too honourable for that; other characters may be, too. Leaving them tied up and wounded would be arguably less humane than a mercy killing, though. Someone might realise that any defeated barbarian knows the area better than they do and could be a guide to the Swamp, if they could communicate with him. That would only postpone the final decision of his fate, however. The Games Master could frame the debate as a social conflict, but it may be easy enough to resolve by other means. In any case, this episode will further illustrate the morals of the various adventurers.

Once the characters have regrouped and tended to any injuries, they have another hour or more to the Swamp before the terrain ahead changes.

BRAVING THE DEAD SWAMP

In the distance, the party can see a haze developing as the land very slowly slopes down, then flattens. Finally they come upon their next landmark: two twisted and very old trees, standing like sentinels at the edge of the Dead Swamp. Each is a man's height in diameter, with hardly any green at the top, yet no signs of rot or weakness. Their knurled roots claw the earth even as their many branches rake the sky like talons. Their bark is hard and smooth but with scars and fissures bearing witness to their great age, and is so dark a grey as to be almost black. At once majestic and malevolent to behold, these trees are in fact harmless, though the land beyond is not.

This is a place to try one's soul, and no mistake. Mud pits and pools of murky water abound, with almost no normal, solid ground. Thick mats of moss blend with pond scum, making it difficult to discern solid surfaces from liquid; base movement speed is halved here. Strange trees grow from the water, whilst others push up from black earth. The canopy of leaves is thin and spotty, but the sun seems muted anyhow. Thin mist rises above eye level and lends

> ## PUSHY, PUSHY...
>
> Many events in this scenario present natural opportunities for a character to shove a rival or hated enemy into harm's way:
>
> - Fending off coyotes
> - Fighting barbarians
> - Avoiding a venomous snake
> - Battling a swamp devil
> - Scaling a narrow mountain trail
> - Defending against a wyvern
> - Barging through a waterfall
> - Stumbling in water amidst bats
> - Teetering above a pit of spikes
> - Clashing with skeletal guardians
> - Arguing with moralising companions
>
> An adventurer so inclined must weigh the risk of getting caught, and its repercussions, against the possibility for complete success, plus the chance that another opportunity might not arise. Revenge attacks might come not only from a survivor but also from his allies—the latter even in the case of complete success—and even the attacker's friends might turn on her over such a dastardly act.
>
> The bad blood between Tobias and Finiel is on-going and may require repeated interventions by the characters. Even if he is the instigator, Tobias always plays the victim in these tussles, agreeing to stop all hostilities if Finiel would just leave him alone. He will use any attack on him as evidence that Finiel is the villain who killed Zarand and is now after him. Meanwhile, Finiel is proud and self-righteous, but will pretend to be reasonable or forgiving to wait for a better chance at Tobias later on.
>
> Such a push should be treated as a surprise attack (MYTHRAS, page 105), with the victim's Perception or Insight used to mitigate its effects. Instead of a push, a really bold or angry character might prefer a blow from a weapon.

a strange, dingy cast to the light in this place. The atmosphere is close and reeks of sulphur and decay. It is unwise to venture into such country—which is exactly why Hessaret used it as a hideout.

The Dead Swamp is demoralising and dank, but far from dead. In fact, here mosquitoes and snakes abound. Some of the latter are large and venomous; a bitten character or animal will get sick, but probably not die. A character from Advent or the frontier region may check Locale to recall the habits and nature of such snakes, helping her compatriots to avoid or spot them. The latter requires a Hard Perception roll, but can be augmented by Survival. Overall, the snakes are not especially aggressive and will attack a large animal or human only defensively, preferring to hide or flee. The biggest problem is stepping on or near one by accident. They can move quickly, but mostly lie very still and may get to attack by surprise. A startled horse or mule might rear or gallop off, and a snake bite could render even a large animal lame.

Beyond normal Fatigue checks, on this leg of the trip, each adventurer must make an unopposed Endurance roll each day, or suffer an extra level of fatigue from breathing the foetid, clammy air and feeding the biting insects.

The Survival skill is vital if the party somehow loses its food, water, or sleeping gear—or its way (see Getting Lost). As mentioned, there are few dry spots, and adventurers who have to sleep on wet ground will suffer from exposure, unless someone succeeds with Survival on their behalf. (A character could use Meditation to good effect.) There is some green brush that will burn, poorly and smokily. Success with Survival yields a modicum of potable water that does not need to be boiled. There are frogs, snakes, slugs, turtles, and edible plants to be found, but they may need to be eaten raw, depending on how well the fire turns out.

From the two menacing trees at the entrance to the swamp, it is a full day's march to the campsite at the centre, if the party makes no missteps. This means that if the explorers arrive at the trees in the middle of the day, they will run out of daylight before reaching a good place to sleep. As daylight begins to fade, the characters should appreciate their situation and may opt to push their movement rate and risk Fatigue, rather than spend a night in the mire. The Games Master should encourage this, because the campsite is meant to be experienced at night. Of course, it might take a profoundly lost party until the end of the *next* day to arrive at the campsite.

Swamp Devil Ambush

Here and there throughout the wetland lurk malevolent elementals known as swamp devils. Each is possessive of its particular patch of ground, attacking any intruder whose footfalls disturb it. They generally keep away from each other, so probably only one is encountered at a time—though there could be a few such encounters, at the Games Master's preference. They do not stalk intruders, but once engaged they do give chase. Adventurers find it difficult to flee quickly in this terrain, but the devils, of course, have no trouble.

Remember that an elemental is immune to normal damage. Thus, the only Non-Player Characters who can hurt a swamp devil are Arkannad and, perhaps surprisingly, Tobias. It may take the party a round to realise that regular attacks do no harm. Arkannad is generally unwilling to use his magic for other characters, but in a desperate situation, he might be persuaded to do so. Running away could save lives (but, as mentioned, it is not easy).

Getting Lost

Hessaret's barbarians used a meandering path of hummocks and patches of solid ground, and any skilled adventurer likewise follows this natural course. The characters have the map to guide them, but this is no guarantee of success. The crude map confers upon any unskilled user the equivalent of Navigation (Dead Swamp) at base ability; for anyone using Track or an appropriate Navigation skill, the map makes checks one grade easier. However, on any fumble, the company is lost and travelling in circles. Feel free to throw in additional swamp devils in this circumstance, though this sort of error should cost the adventurers time, not their lives.

Getting lost puts everyone on edge and brings down obloquy on the pathfinder, who probably gets replaced. On the other hand, whoever gets the company back on track earns hearty praise.

The Haunted Campsite

Eventually, the party arrives at Hessaret's final campsite, which is in a stand of withered, twisted trees on a low rocky rise, just beyond the centre of the swamp. This place offers dry ground and firewood; the characters would be crazy not to bed down here. Of course, this is also where the bloody slave uprising occurred so the night will be filled with unrest and ghostly visitations.

Inspection of the site reveals a lack of healthy vegetation and some remarkably round stones, which turn out to be human skulls half buried in the earth. Further investigation yields corroded bits of weapons, armour, tools, utensils, and cooking gear. This was surely an ancient camp, and a pitched battle was waged here—but Hessaret met his doom at Advent.... The characters may speculate as desired about the grim artefacts.

Those taking the first watch that night are the victims of the Haunts that are bound to this ghastly place.

There are more than enough spirits here to afflict each character. First, an adventurer notices faint sights at the corner of her eye, then suddenly, faint sounds of human voices pleading, sobbing, or shrieking. Slowly and dramatically, these sights and sounds coalesce into gruesome death scenes. A man in rags wrestles a guard to the ground, and two women rush forward to brain him with stones. A prisoner tries to parry a sword stroke but is run through and gurgles as he falls. A woman pleads for mercy but is decapitated, her head rolling over the character's foot. A barbarian is chased down by four slaves and chopped to pieces by their axes. Some of the apparitions seem unaware of the characters, whilst others beg them for help, threaten them, or scream, "You do not belong here!"

After a few minutes of this, each character is assaulted by Miasma (Mythras, page 150), and if his nerve fails he runs screaming into the night, into the swamp. Obviously, this could be very dangerous. At least a shrieking character is easier to find in the dark.

When things have calmed down, a character making an appropriate Lore roll, or a Herculean Locale roll, recalls some old tale about a slave revolt against their cruel barbarian masters somewhere in the region, and may even associate it with tales of Hessaret. The spooky madness experienced at the campsite does not necessarily need to be tied to anything, though.

THE NAMELESS HILL

Departing in the morning, after a restless night (check Fatigue), the company now needs the second (Finiel's) half of the treasure map. Another day of trudging to another huge boulder (this one split in half, as if by a god's chisel) has them leaving the swamp, which should improve everyone's mood. In the morning, they head even farther southeast over more prairie towards some hills rising from a light forest. At first, the characters may not be able to discern the hills very well, as they are about 10 kilometres from the edge of the swamp and there is fog in the morning, but after some time they become confident that the map is not leading them astray. The tallest of these hills, which has no name amongst the civilised people near Advent, is not particularly tall (175 metres) and cannot really be called a mountain, though it is rather steep.

Travelling across this solid ground is unremarkable, so the party should make good time to the edge of the forest, and skirting the bases of the smaller ones, the adventurers discover a large pond where they may replenish their flasks, water their animals, or even bathe. Resting in this tranquil spot to dispel fatigue seems like a good idea, but will take time, and actually is not so safe (see "Wyvern Attack"). The crystal-clear pond is fed by a waterfall pouring from the

FINIEL'S PORTION OF THE MAP

southeast face of the tallest hill; there is no visible stream or other outlet, so why the pond does not overflow is a mystery. It is also odd to see a waterfall emanating from a hill, rather than from a river atop a cliff. Surely the gods were at work in the creation of this singular place.

The nomads and barbarians of the Long Riding recognise the sanctity of this site and stay away. Gods aside, they know that it is too dangerous to linger here due to the wyverns that nest in the hills.

The adventurers are primed to look, so it should not take them long to find the faded trail at the base of the hill. A successful Perception roll or Track at Easy grade does the trick. Treat this as a team test (MYTHRAS, page 52). Failures lead to wasted time and yet more opportunity for squabbling.

The trail presents a treacherous single-file climb along the north face of the hill, about 1.2 metres wide mostly, but less than a metre in some places. Any other approach would be even worse; there is no other way up. The steep trail is broken ground, with crumbling pebbly soil, occasional shrub roots, and patches of weeds and lichen. To the left is the hillside; to the right, a steep rocky drop. A mount or pack animal can be led up this track, but only slowly and with great care. As an alternative, leaving the animals to forage and drink near the edge of the pond seems safe enough in this remote place. In fact, there is no safe spot for the animals at all.

The company may want to assign a new point person at this stage. Having a rival at your back is a serious concern here. The adventurers may be put as a buffer between the two factions of Non-Player Characters, for safety's sake. Tobias and Arkannad will try to take the lead, but this is open for debate.

Before they even get started up the trail, there are some sun-bleached bones in plain sight, which the characters should investigate to their hearts' content.

In ascending the trail, each adventurer must make three Athletics rolls, once each at about one quarter, half, and three quarters of the way, with half her armour penalty subtracted from base movement. Any failure means the whole party is held up. Again, failures add up to delays, and climbing this trail in fading light can only be worse. Any fumble means the character has fallen; use discretion in deciding how badly. A Luck Point may be used to re-roll Athletics or grab a shrub projecting from the cliff face. If someone's beast slips and falls, there is nothing to do but let it go.

Remember that Loram is not only huge and ungainly, but also afraid of heights. This may lead to him freezing at some point, unable to advance or retreat. A contest of Influence versus Passion, modified according to whoever attempts the soothing (probably Finiel), can restore Loram's mobility. Mules are famous for stubbornness, so if one decides to stop on the trail it could be even more trouble than Loram.

Nervous characters might tie themselves together, but this could lead to disaster—especially considering that Loram, the heaviest one, is the most likely to slip.

IS THAT WHAT I THINK IT IS?

Recall the background reading. Though none of the slave's family ever managed to mount a quest for the hoard, over the years, a few bold parties have attempted to claim it. Bones and items from these ill-fated ventures decorate various spots on and in Nameless Hill. The Games Master should point them out freely, for atmosphere.

For example, near the foot of the trail, at several points early on the path, and looking down over the edge, one finds remains not only of people but of animals—but almost none of the skeletons seem to be complete. Those with training in anatomy or another appropriate Lore notice deep scratches in large bones, and long bones snapped in the middle, as if by extreme force. One mule skull has been cracked in half like a walnut. An empty bronze helmet has been staved in from above, such that it is nearly inverted. A Critical Perception role uncovers a broken piece of bone that has been driven straight through a ruined buckler—wait, not a bone, but a broken tooth.

Falling or infighting amongst treasure hunters cannot explain all of these findings, but an attack by a giant monster can. Working this out before the wyverns come could save lives.

WYVERN ATTACK

Some tribes of the Long Riding call this place Wyvern Rock, but never speak of it to outsiders due to the sacredness of the site. There is always a mated pair of wyverns nesting in a deep cave on the far side of the hill, and today the male attacks the adventurers as they edge up the narrow trail, at about the three-quarter point. This beast is motivated by hunger and territoriality, and so is not inclined to fight to the death. However, if it becomes so badly injured that it cannot escape, it stops at nothing to stay alive. Remember its Frenzy ability!

The character on point is attacked first. The wyvern swoops in from above; each adventurer is allowed a Perception roll to negate surprise. If the party has solved the mystery of the bones littering the hill, then this Perception roll will be Easy. Unless someone succeeds in an appropriate Lore check, the company might misidentify a wyvern as a dragon.

Wyverns see well at night, an advantage over most prey. For an extra challenge, the Games Master might want to arrange this combat as night falls. Considering the distances travelled this day, it may well be dusk when the attack comes.

The beast fights from the air unless such becomes impossible, charging through contact with either of its attacks. Experience has taught it that a fall will kill its prey, and it can use either Bite or Tail Sweep towards this end. Its Tail Sweep might affect more than one victim. Otherwise, its tactic is to bite a character, lift her off the hillside, and drop her to her doom, leaving a tenderised corpse for later.

It is imperative that a grabbed character keep from falling by further grabbing or somehow lashing herself to the beast. To resist being snatched by the monster the character could try to hold onto the hill, or a comrade might be able to grab her and pull her back, but this had better be quick, before the wyvern lifts her out of reach. Of course, killing the beast that is carrying a character off leads to a deadly fall. Spending a Luck Point enables such a character to land on top of the relatively soft wyvern instead of the ground.

The adventurers have a tactical quandary: Hurting the monster's wings would neutralise its chief advantage, but removing its ability to fly away would force it to stay and fight longer. To drive it away, they are better off aiming for a key location. Success with Lore (Monsters) or Lore (Strategy and Tactics) at Hard grade reveals this. Ranged weapons or long spears are very useful here.

Remember, the characters are fighting on a narrow ledge, requiring an Athletics or Acrobatics check of anyone under attack. Any fumbled Athletics, Acrobatics, or Evade roll means the character has slipped and now clings—for the moment—to the crumbling edge of the path. Special effects in combat also should be chosen with this setting in mind. Appropriate situational modifiers for close combat (MYTHRAS, page 101) include attacking in a confined

situation, defending against a mounted (flying) foe, and fighting while on unstable ground, any of which inflicts a penalty grade of Hard. Also, don't forget to check for Fatigue.

If the adventurers have brought their animals up the trail, these poor beasts will certainly begin to panic when combat ensues. They might rear and plunge, or slip and fall off the cliff, or try to turn and run back down the trail. A nearby character might be trampled or bashed over the edge or against the cliff wall. On the other hand, after its initial attack, the wyvern might go for an animal instead of a human and fly away satisfied with a bigger meal.

Either Tobias or Finiel might take advantage of the confusion of melee to get in a pot-shot at the other, probably at range. Such a sneak attack becomes less likely if the fight is not going well, in which case every sword counts. Of course, it is an easy choice not to interfere with a monster that is doing the dirty work for you.

This encounter provides a clear indication of each combatant's mettle to everyone involved—information that could be very valuable later in a tight spot. Any single fighter who drives off (or even holds his own against) the wyvern is obviously formidable; the Games Master might choose to point this out at an appropriate moment.

Feel free to have this beast's statistically identical mate attack, too, if the company seems to be having too easy a time—or save it for the return trip down the hill. (This is probably too much for most parties, though.)

Wyverns love to eat horses or mules, so the mate tries to carry off some of the party's chattel left down below, even if characters up above defend themselves successfully. Since the foot of the trail is out of sight around the shoulder of the hill, the company would not discover this loss for some time. Local nomads and barbarians value their animals too much to brave this watering hole, unless absolutely desperate.

It is possible that only some members of the party go ahead to scout out the trail, leaving the rest behind with the animals. (Loram, for example, would jump at the chance not to go up so high—though he would not reveal why he was so willing to stay behind.) Such a division of the company would probably spell disaster: Fewer swords would then be pitted against each of the two monsters, possibly leading to a "total party kill". To avoid this, the Games Master may prefer to omit the second wyvern attacking down below. Of course, any group about to head up the trail has the chance to investigate all those bones, before committing, and this should give pause to even the most reckless adventurer.

Should anyone care to investigate, a dangerous climb to the wyverns' cave yields a clutch of three leathery eggs, each the size of a small melon. They will hatch in a few months, if kept only slightly warmer than ambient temperature. If kept viable, these eggs would fetch quite a price back in The Vale. The female wyvern may well be guarding them, especially if she has not already been encountered.

Misty Falls

After two hours (but possibly more) of climbing from the base of Nameless Hill, the company discovers that the trail ends abruptly at a wall of water. The actual mouth of the waterfall is about 10 metres farther up the mountain. Far below, the bottom 10 metres of the falls are concealed by heavy mist. The sound here is deafening; even loud shouts are barely audible. An adventurer must make a Formidable Perception check to hear properly, unless someone speaks directly into her ear. This is, therefore, an ideal place to backstab or push someone to his fate unnoticed.

When reaching the top, each character must attempt an Athletics or Acrobatics check due to the suddenly slippery rocks underfoot. Keep rolling until success or fumble, which means the hapless explorer has slipped and will fall 150 metres to the foot of the mountain. Probably (1–4 on 1d6) he lands in the water with no harm, unless he cannot swim, at which point he might drown without help. Otherwise (5 or 6) he almost certainly is heavily injured by landing on the rocks and will die without rapid aid. Spending a Luck Point here guarantees landing in the water. In either case, due to the heavy mist, the landing spot of the falling character is a mystery to his companions above. Even the sound of the landing is probably obscured.

It should not take long for someone to realise that the trail probably continues behind the falls. Check for Insight only if the players are really stuck (which seems unlikely).

The Hidden Caverns

The entrance to the caverns is behind the dense sheet of water; a team test of Perception is required to find exactly where it is best to cross. Pushing through requires a contest of Strength (Mythras, page 39) against the crush of the falling water, which for this purpose has Brawn 60% and damage modifier +1d4. Failure means the adventurer

> ### LIGHTING THE DARKNESS
>
> The caverns beyond the Misty Falls are either very dark or pitch black. Finiel's lantern is of great use and Loram has two torches, even if other characters have not thought to bring any. Stumbling through the water and being plagued by bats make it challenging to keep the lights burning. Magical lighting would be a godsend. All Perception rolls should be penalised depending on the lighting, but an adventurer carrying a light source incurs no penalty to see close objects.

cannot penetrate the wall of water and has been knocked back or down; a fumble means she is swept away, down into the pool (but not onto the rocks) far below. A brawny character could help by pulling or pushing a weaker one, but a pushed individual might not interpret this as "help".

A Formidable Perception check reveals an easier way, around the edge of the waterfall, requiring only a normal Athletics or Acrobatics roll. Whether that Perception roll occurs before someone tries to crash through the water is up to the Games Master.

If any animals have been brought up the mountainside and survived the wyvern assault, presumably they will be left at this point. Really, trying to bring a horse into a cave, never mind through a waterfall or around such a slippery bend, would be pure folly.

BATS IN THE OUTER CHAMBER

Following the cavern into the hill leads the company into a large space filled with waist-deep water, fed by another small waterfall and drained via crevices. Struggling across the room (wading, or Swimming at Easy grade) brings them to a path leading up next to the second waterfall. Noticing this path could be difficult, depending on the lighting; in daylight, it would be obvious. The sound of crashing water gets quieter as the adventurers proceed across the chamber, with Perception checks no longer penalised near the path.

This Outer Chamber is home to a colony of bats—the usual insectivorous type, though rather large (wingspan 0.5 metres). These creatures are not a danger themselves and are not meant to be fought, but they cause trouble nonetheless. When disturbed by noise or light, the thousands of bats take flight en masse, zooming past the company to depart the cave via small, unseen passages in the roof near the Misty Falls. This causes quite a din and confusion for a solid 5 minutes. Characters might drop light sources into the water, fall, or become otherwise disoriented. A failed Willpower check (unopposed, unless the adventurer has a relevant phobia or other Passion) indicates panic and necessitates an Athletics check to keep from stumbling and dousing a light. Fumbling the Willpower roll makes the Athletics roll Formidable, and such a panicky character suffers the same penalty to other skill checks as well.

Anyone who is not distracted and can see well enough may attack a rival by surprise. The water here is deep enough to conceal a body (though it would tend to float, unless weighted...by armour, say). There are a few skeletons with ruined gear at rest in the water. A panicked character without Swim might be plagued by momentary drowning, easily overcome by any intervention.

A Critical Perception roll indicates that an adventurer has literally stumbled upon two huge planks sunk in the water near the path. Shod with bronze end caps and bands and being about 2 metres by 30 centimetres by 6 centimetres, each beam is massive and still quite sturdy, having been rubbed in some sort of fat to keep the water out. The reason they are here is unclear...for now.

The company might elect to change the point person here. It is important to know exactly who is in front, considering what comes next.

PITFALL TRAP

The sounds of the Misty Falls fade almost to silence as the company traverses the path to a steep passage that ascends another 6 metres, terminating abruptly in a 6-metre fall into a pit lined with 30-centimetre bronze stakes. Considering the skill and dedication of its barbarian engineers plus the unique character of the natural passageway, this trap is deadly.

- Purpose: Death
- Trigger: Stepping off the edge of an unseen cliff
- Difficulty: 80%
- Resistance: Perception (at penalty, according to lighting)—not Evade
- Effect: 2d6 falling damage to each of 2 Hit Locations, plus each location lands on 1d3 spikes at base 1d3 damage each; the Impale special effect is automatic and a critical Difficulty result yields a further special effect of Ignore Armour for one of the stakes

At least (but probably only) the leading character is affected. Success in Acrobatics knocks 2 metres off of the effective falling distance and reduces the damage

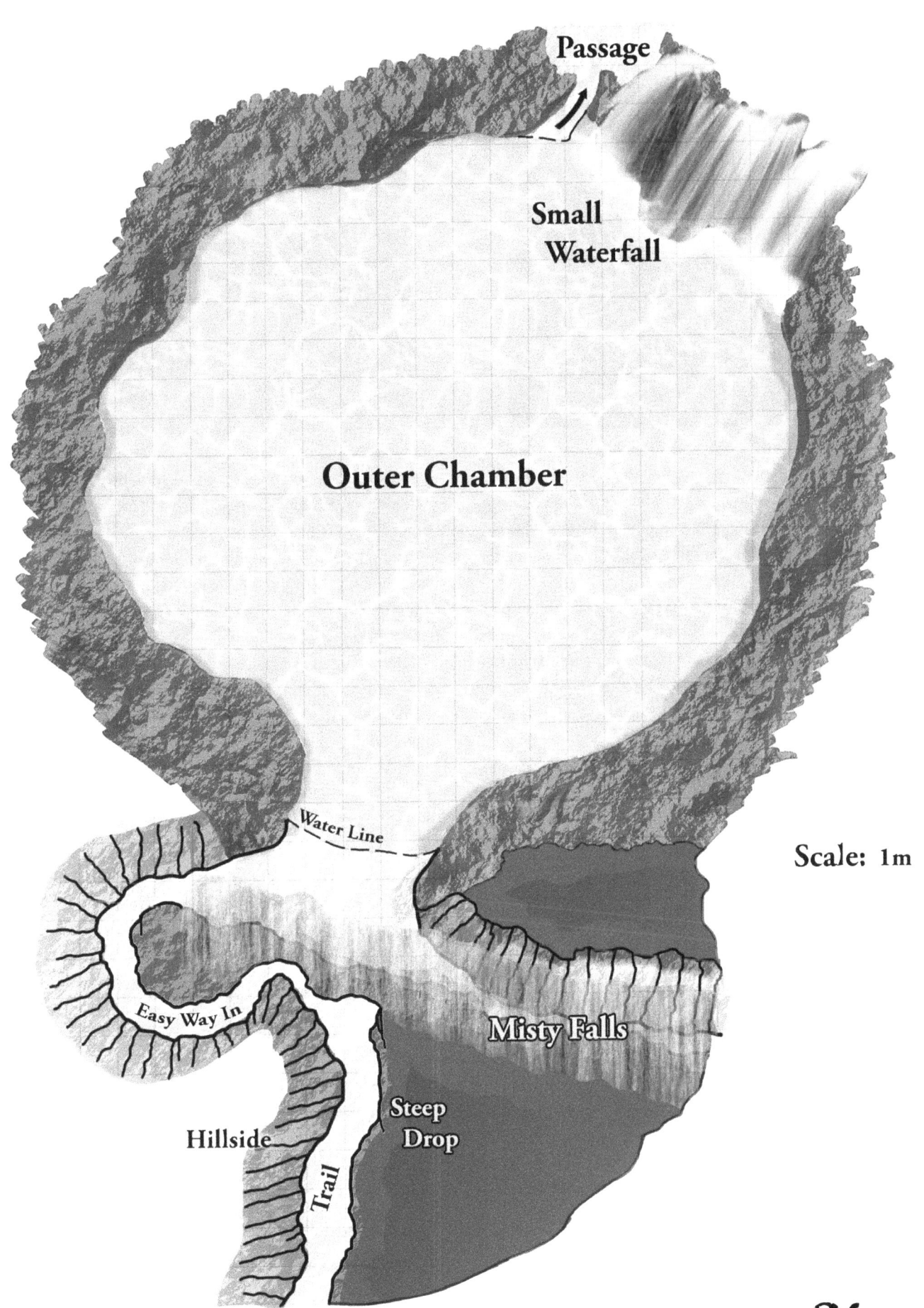

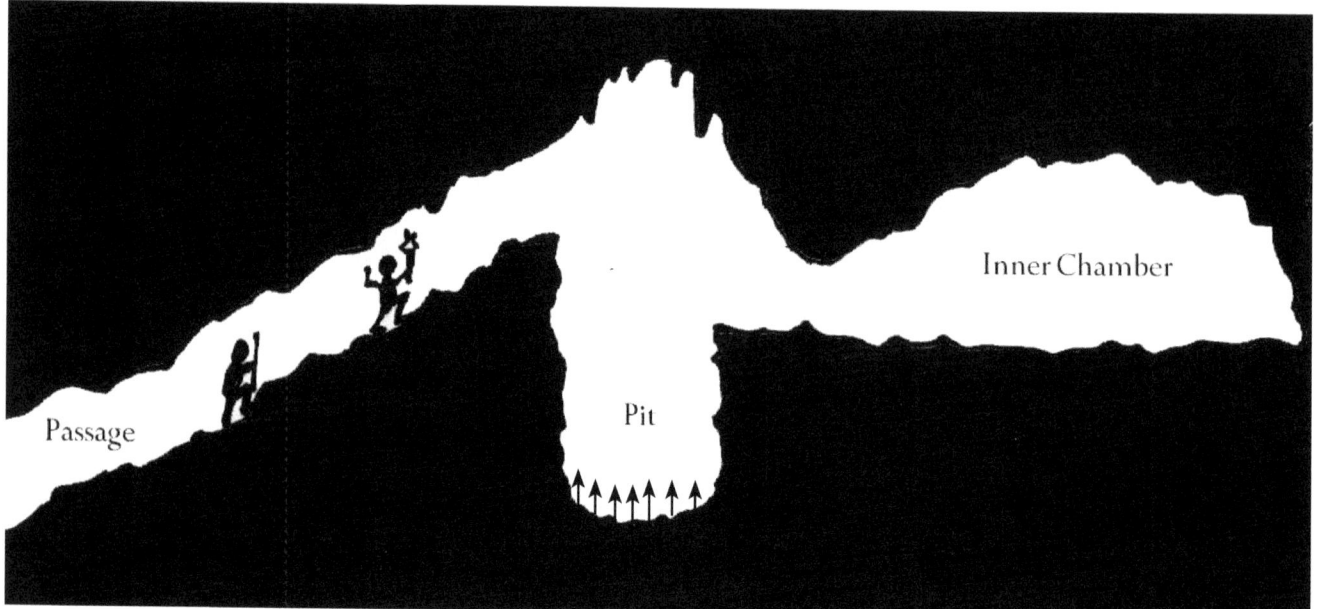

accordingly, but does not reduce the stake damage. Conversely, armour does not protect against the fall, but does against the stakes. An impaled adventurer may be unable to lift herself off the spikes—for example, if she lands face-up on her back (Chest or Abdomen location). A victim landing on her head is almost certain to die.

Characters still up in the passageway may attempt to climb down the sheer side (Athletics, at double armour penalty); a fumble results in a fall from some fraction of the 6-metre height and impalement. Obviously, climbing gear is very helpful here and could make the difference between life and death.

The pit is 4 metres long and 3 metres wide, with sheer sides. A few dramatically mangled skeletons decorate the bottom. To get out of the pit, a character must either climb back up 6 metres from whence he came or forge ahead and walk to the far end, climbing up only 4 metres to a small (1.5 metres deep by 2 metres wide) ledge that leads to another chamber. Merely walking across the bottom of the pit is dangerous, due to the uneven natural floor and the profusion of bronze stakes. Each walker must make an unopposed Athletics check to avoid tripping and becoming impaled upon 1d3 stakes in some location.

A successful Perception roll reveals what seems to be a groove running the length of the pit along the right side. The groove is about 6 centimetres tall and 6 centimetres deep, and has been carved just above the height of the stakes. This should ring a bell if someone discovered those planks under the water in the Outer Chamber, and even if nobody did, an Insight roll now gives the idea that there must have been some way for the designers of this pit to traverse it safely. Beyond that, it is up to the players to realise that the water in the cave might conceal something. A character revisiting the Outer Chamber with the intent to search for something in the water need only make a Hard Perception roll to discover the planks, which fit neatly into the groove and will support a person easily. Also, perhaps one could find some other interesting way to use the groove to cross the room more safely.

The ceiling in this place is quite high. An overconfident or slightly psychotic athlete (Arkannad will do this, and it is dramatically appropriate for him to succeed if he is a Non-Player Character) could take a running leap from the passage to land on the small ledge at the far side. This would be foolhardy yet extremely impressive if successful. Anyone accomplishing that feat would surely be seen as fearsome, and fearless, by his companions—which later could provide some Insight in a tense situation. Again, the Games Master might choose to point this out at the right time.

The Inner Chamber and the Guardians of the Hoard

The low exit from the pit leads into this roughly circular cave, which is silent.

Eight skeleton warriors stand motionless across the room, evenly spaced in two rows, eternally waiting to pounce on robbers. Each bears an unadorned but serviceable bronze hoplite cuirass plus helm, a hoplite shield, and a broadsword, all covered in verdigris by the passage of time and not at all shiny. They attack, possibly by surprise, when the first interloper enters the middle of the chamber. Characters may check Perception, penalised as usual for imperfect lighting.

These sleepless magical watchdogs were created by the shaman Mōdant. They are the remains of loyal bandits who fell in battle, were reanimated with their self-same Spirits of Undeath, and are still faithful to their leader and his charge to guard this place forever. Of course, they would let Hessaret or Mōdant pass, but those men are long gone.

The skeletons attack ceaselessly.

There is only one way out: the same way the company entered. A fleeing character might fail to recall the pit that waits 1.5 metres beyond the exit. This time, roll Evade instead of Perception; the check is one grade easier if the character remembers in time, but one grade harder (for no net effect) if he is running or sprinting. The fall from this side is only 4 metres, not 6 metres, but the stakes are still there, as are the dangerous walk across and climb at the other end. The guardians will chase intruders into the pit (but not beyond) and can clamber down the walls and walk among the stakes quite nimbly, with no net armour penalties, thanks to their lack of flesh. Thus, the pit is even more dangerous than the adventurers probably thought.

If eight seems inappropriate, some other number of these horrors may be selected by the Games Master. They are meant to be a deadly challenge, considering what they guard and the temperament of the men who put them there.

As earlier on the hillside trail, Tobias and Finiel will likely take advantage of melee confusion to try to backstab one another. Considering the threat at hand, though, this seems very unwise. Circumstances might require an opposed roll of Insight versus Passion to exercise good judgement.

HESSARET'S TREASURE

Assuming the skeleton warriors have been defeated, the party has the opportunity to look around properly and realises that this chamber is in fact a *tomb*. Hessaret's "greatest treasure" was of course his true love, Bōdda. He and her father Mōdant laid her to rest in highest honour inside this natural wonder of a mountain and set the retinue of skeletons as her eternal guard.

Faded glyphs and paintings decorate the rear wall. A low stone table (a shrine to Renamos, with appropriate runes) bears a stylised oil lamp, chalice, and small bust of a beautiful woman, all made of gold. On the wall directly behind the shrine hangs a great bear skin at the centre of a display of decorative long spears.

The extinct Grestet were forebears of Arkannad's Kirstet clan. He does not know enough lore to realise this, but the glyphs, trappings, and overall style of the tomb are eerily familiar to him from the common traditions that persist amongst his own people. Success with Insight means Arkannad sees that he has much more in common with the reviled bandits than his civilised companions, who suddenly are would-be tomb robbers.

A stone sarcophagus stands behind the shrine, between it and the wall. Its lid bears an artfully carved effigy of a female warrior (Bōdda), the same woman depicted in the bust. The contents of this coffin are not to be missed—but it is not clear that the party will open it.

The Company Disintegrates

The following events need to be handled step by step, though they occur rapidly. Passions will dominate the reactions of the Non-Player Characters and, perhaps, those of the characters as well.

There is no need to check whether Arkannad has been affected by his cultural taboo against tomb robbing; for him, resisting would be Hopeless. He implores his companions to leave the chamber immediately and forget the treasure. "This is a tomb, a holy place. We should not have trespassed. This is wrong. This is evil!" Check his Influence, boosted by his Passion. Even a character unaffected by his pleas should be able to see that Arkannad is deadly serious.

Although he does not share Arkannad's cultural sensibilities, Loram too may have a problem with robbing any grave, even a barbarian's. Check his Hatred of breaking social rules, unopposed at first, at Hard grade because this involves a foreign culture and so is generally less objectionable. Others may need to make similar checks.

For Finiel and Tobias, though, there is no need to check. They have risked life and limb on a quest for treasure; they covet wealth in general; they are selfish; and, after all, this woman was only a barbarian. The Games Master could rule that a fumbled Passion or Willpower check means even Finiel's cold heart is affected and she changes her mind about robbing the place, but for dramatic purposes, Tobias must not change his mind.

Likely, Finiel scolds any character who balks: "Oh, grow up! This stuff isn't doing any good here in a cave. Everyone who ever cared about it is long forgotten. It's worth a fortune! Don't lose your nerve now." Tobias actually backs her up here, in his calm, calculated way: "She's right, lads. No sense leaving empty-handed, after all we've been through."

Now Arkannad has his own chance (again, boosted by his Passion) to persuade Loram and everyone else: "Don't do it. The dead must be left to rest in peace, as the living intended."

The simplest way to handle all this is to treat it as social conflict (MYTHRAS, page 287), pitting Arkannad against Finiel and Tobias in an attempt to persuade Loram not to loot Bōdda's tomb. Use discretion in deciding whose skills will be used for base rolls and whose supporting skills or Passions might augment them. Opinionated characters may also speak up to augment one plea or the other, while the undecided may be swayed one way or the other like Loram. Players should retain the right to decide what their characters do, but faithful roleplaying should affect those decisions and should observe the results of this conflict.

Finally, someone, at the very least Tobias, begins to take the items from the shrine or starts to pry up the lid of the sarcophagus. Check Arkannad's clan Loyalty to see how he will further react: Failure means he merely refuses to join in, instead abandoning the company for parts unknown, but success means he fights anyone attempting to defile the tomb! Count this attack as a surprise to anyone failing at Insight.

At this point, a battle royal could erupt. The possibilities are too numerous to detail. Some obvious options for any character:

- Attack an enemy, either head-on or stealthily from behind.
- Put your back to a wall and only defend yourself.
- Quietly swipe an accessible item.
- Exit the chamber, either to depart like Arkannad or lie in wait for survivors.

Nasty Surprises

Finiel now makes a concerted move against Tobias, from behind if at all possible—which should be easy if he is already engaged with someone else, such as Arkannad. Even if both have survived all of the preceding dangers, it is exceedingly likely that they now engage in a battle to the death. Finiel still has an ally in Loram, while Arkannad has either abandoned or turned on Tobias. The question then becomes, how many of the characters will recall the sack of gold Tobias promised for protection and rush to his aid? If Tobias comes out on top, he will not hesitate to kill Finiel. It is difficult to envision a realistic endgame in which both Finiel and Tobias survive. To achieve this, both would have to remain trussed for the entire journey back to civilisation, only to have their blood feud play out in another place as soon as they were set free.

If earlier in the adventure, someone fell yet survived, he could dramatically return now to wreak havoc by surprise. Consider the timing, though: swimming to shore, climbing back up the trail, and penetrating the caverns would take over 2 hours. This character instead might be encountered on the narrow trail, as others descend. If Loram is the one making a comeback, then he definitely does not climb up, but simply hides near the bottom with his great hammer ready.

Inside the Sarcophagus

The sarcophagus holds the remains of Bōdda, clad in a fantastically ornate panoply of scale mail chased with gold and embellished with gems. The sword on her breast is likewise decorated. There are rings on her withered fingers and bracelets on her wrists. Most breath-taking of all, however, is her golden funerary mask, with features limned in unfaded black and crimson. Even the most jaded fortune hunter must catch his breath at this sight. A king could not expect a finer burial. One wonders if knowing this would have softened any character's stance against looting.

Returning to Civilisation

No matter the other details, obviously any adventurer who is not going to die here must leave the mountain. The Games Master should consider carefully the points below:

- Survivors may either loot the tomb or just depart. Do they leave dead comrades to rot in someone else's tomb? Where and how will they bury the dead?
- Considering the challenges beyond, a character with a Serious Wound to the leg is in real danger of never making it out of the Inner Chamber. Waiting around for natural healing is not an option, unless someone has brought weeks' worth of food and water. Thus, wounding an opponent's leg and leaving basically consigns her to a slow, painful death. On the other hand, even if no single adventurer has brought enough provisions, pooling *everybody's* resources might be sufficient to keep one person alive. Fetching help from Advent is also an option, though a time-consuming one.
- Who leaves first? Success with Insight or Lore (Strategy and Tactics) reveals that racing to get out and down first is advantageous for setting an ambush.
- If there is a race, who crosses the bottom of the pit first? Who first ascends 6 metres to the passage? That is the single key spot to hold, from a strategic point of view, as nobody can escape the caverns without passing it. Success with Lore (Strategy and Tactics) makes this clear; success with Insight reveals what someone

else has in mind in general. Caving in the ceiling at that spot is an efficient and merciless way to slow or stop rivals—possibly even permanently.

- Is it day or night when the characters emerge from the caverns? Descending the trail after dark seems like a bad idea, but may seem a better option than spending the night in the caverns.
- Dropping a sack of treasure down Misty Falls saves a lot of effort on the trail, but retrieval requires swimming. Of course, a drop into the pool is also the fastest way down, for a bag of loot or a character, but is the risk of injury too great?
- Is a wyvern (or two) still ready to battle the returning adventurers?
- Is a character waiting to ambush those still descending the trail?
- At the bottom of the hill, how many pack animals have been chased away or devoured?
- Why follow the same trail home? From what the adventurers have seen on the map and in their travels, they could minimise time spent in the Dead Swamp, or even avoid it altogether. The distance is greater, but the travelling is so much easier and safer that it is definitely worthwhile. Even novice outdoorsmen will find it difficult to get badly lost, as this region is bounded on the northwest by rivers that will lead them eventually to Advent. Success with Navigation (Open Country) keeps one on the quickest path, or the easiest—character's choice.
- On the way home through The Wilds, will the characters meet more barbarian patrols or coyotes?

CONCLUSION

It is envisioned that each character gains 3 Experience Rolls from this adventure, and possibly, valuable allies, dangerous enemies, or significant wealth. Each should also learn something about trusting strangers, his own scruples, and human nature in general. The notes below could provide the basis for one or more further adventures.

It is assumed that either Finiel or Tobias has died in the course of events; see prior notes. This renders it rather unlikely that the characters will ever know for certain who killed Zarand. The Games Master might have them meet in Advent the person who sold Tobias the mushroom poison, but it could be more interesting to leave the mystery unsolved.

When this business has concluded, a surviving Finiel would leave town, whereas Tobias has great plans and would remain in Advent. In principle, either Tobias or Finiel is interested in continuing a partnership with the characters, unless in the course of the scenario, they have ended up as adversaries. In the absence of his respective boss, though, neither Arkannad nor Loram is interested. If Tobias is gone, Arkannad simply walks off into the sunset. If Finiel has not made it, Loram is despondent and first returns to Advent to drown his sorrows and then travels to a less unfriendly town to enlist as a soldier there.

The characters may opt to stay in Advent, whether or not they want to continue as partners with Tobias. If they have ended up as his adversaries, though, he causes trouble for them at every turn. He could spread vicious rumours about them, for example, or frame them for crimes he has committed, or convince the merchants in town to cheat them or not deal with them at all. He might even acquire some new hirelings to attack them.

The characters could proffer the story of their adventure to Captain Ulster as useful information about The Wilds and perils therein. He is entertained by the tale, but not especially interested in any of the facts. Travellers should stick to the Great Road, which is safe enough. People foolish enough to venture into a place called The Wilds deserve what they get, and it's not his problem. However, he is impressed by the adventurers' gusto and offers them work as mercenaries for scouting missions and the like. They should be quite useful in keeping those savages to the north in line.

The treasure from Bōdda's tomb is fabulous but cannot be sold in Advent. Finding buyers with enough cash and interest requires a trip to a large city, such as Cylder or West Port. The exact monetary values of the lamp, chalice, bust, funerary mask, mail, and sword are left to the imagination of the Games Master. It is clear to anyone, however, that they are worth a lot. If a cash value for the hoard is needed, then a total of 10,000 Silver Pieces is a good place to start: bear in mind though, that selling the pieces will be a major task in itself and is guaranteed to raise suspicions, questions, jealousy and further greed. Characters foolish enough to brag about having such valuable stuff are sure to court unwanted attention.

NPC AND MONSTER STATISTICS

Each Non-Player Character has been given Luck Points as would a Player Character. As The Realm is fairly magic-poor, the Games Master may prefer to increase an individual's spell-casting abilities for use in a different setting.

TOBIAS

This rogue is attractive, with dark brown hair, striking green eyes, a nice nose, good skin, and straight teeth. He also tries to dress well. He seems open and friendly—a classic confidence man. Tobias is 30 years old and not physically imposing (175 centimetres, 78 kilograms).

Tobias grew up in Cylder and tried to establish a criminal career there, but ran afoul of Kardesh Weathervane and wisely fled to safer climes. He does not talk much about that chapter of his life. After proving himself in Advent by killing a local tough over a crooked dice game, Zarand took him in as a partner, but was always slightly distant with him. Tobias remains bitter about that; he is certain that Zarand never really trusted him, which annoys his vanity. In recent months, Tobias has established a successful protection racket, shaking down intimidated travellers who are keen to avoid trouble from the likes of Arkannad and Loram.

Although he speaks calmly and quietly, and has a knack for telling people what they want to hear; this villain is unscrupulous and ruthless. There is nothing he will not do to attain what he desires. Vile deeds such as murder and tomb robbing mean nothing to him. When he overheard that Zarand was right about the treasure map, he did not hesitate in planning his boss's demise. He is not trustworthy, and as a result, he distrusts others, assuming that everyone has an angle and is working it at all times, just as he does. He is slightly overconfident and self-important. Tobias' idiom is depraved selfishness, duplicity, and borderline cowardice. He does not care much for adventuring, but sees it as a means to an end.

His on-going chief goal is to become the boss of Advent, respected or at least feared by all. He had thought to do this via a reputation for violence, backed by his thugs Arkannad and Loram, but the prospect of piles of gleaming treasure has now seized his imagination. He intends to buy his way to the top instead. His other goals include obtaining nice clothes and baubles to appear wealthy and important, and indulging in carnal pleasures.

Tobias' immediate plans: Persuade the characters to support him on the quest. Use them as buffer and glue to keep the group together. Grab and hide as much good stuff from the hoard as possible, when others are distracted. Do away with Finiel or Loram as needed.

He owns mixed armour, a travelling cloak, a short sword, and a dagger concealed in his right boot, plus a Short Bow and arrows. He has spent a lot of money to acquire good-quality hoplite plate, worth 1 extra point in those locations. His money and inessential possessions have been left in Advent. Although he does not really carry much, he is not very strong, so he starts off Burdened. Carrying a lot of treasure would cause his skills to suffer badly.

Equipment: Armour, short sword, dagger, cloak, Short Bow, quiver, 20 arrows, pack, bedroll, water skin, wine skin, rations, thief's toolkit, poison (mushroom), 2 large sacks, heavy silver bracelet (Burdened).

In combat, he stays out of the fray if at all possible, using his bow at range and backstabbing when he can. His weapons will not do much against skeleton warriors. Tobias has one dose left of poison (Mushroom Toxin: Ingested, Potency 75, Resist Endurance, Onset 1d3 rounds, Duration 1 day, Conditions Agony, Asphyxiation, Unconsciousness, Death) for food or drink, but not for smearing on a weapon. He might add it to a wine flask and offer it to a thirsty enemy.

Tobias has also managed to learn Folk Magic, which is unavailable to worshippers of the Founding Four gods and thus would get him into serious social trouble if discovered. Not surprisingly, he keeps this completely secret; none of his compatriots know. Once he got a visiting nomad girl drunk to take advantage of her and persuaded her to part not only with her virtue, but also with Feyr's gift of the Disruption spell. This could be important in any encounter with a Swamp Devil.

Characteristics	Attributes		1d20	Location	AP/HP
STR: 10	Action Points	3	1–3	Right Leg	2/5
CON: 11	Damage Modifier	None	4–6	Left Leg	2/5
SIZ: 12	Magic Points	14	7–9	Abdomen	6/6
DEX: 14	Movement	6m	10–12	Chest	6/7
INT: 15	Initiative Bonus	12	13–15	Right Arm	2/4
POW: 14	Armour	Good hoplite plate cuirass and helm, quilted limbs	16–18	Left Arm	2/4
CHA: 14	Luck Points	3	19–20	Head	6/5
	Folk Magic	38% (Disruption)			

Skills: *Athletics 34%, Brawn 22%, Commerce 76%, Conceal 33%, Courtesy 34%, Customs 77%, Deceit 79%, Endurance 22%, Evade 39%, First Aid 22%, Influence 63%, Insight 50%, Literacy 40%, Native Tongue 79%, Perception 52%, Sleight 43%, Stealth 64%, Streetwise 78%, Swim 21%, Unarmed 24%, Willpower 48%*

Passions: *Selfish 98%, Covet Wealth and Power 69%, Self Important 59%*

Combat Style: *Frontier Rogue (Shortsword, Club, Buckler, Short Bow; Swashbuckling) 45%, Frontier Commoner (Battleaxe, Hatchet, Dagger, Sling) 29%*

Weapon	Size/Force	Reach	Damage	AP/HP
Dagger	S	S	1d4+1	6/8
Club	M	M	1d6	4/4
Shortsword	M	S	1d6	6/8
Buckler	M	S	1d3	6/9
Short Bow	L	-	1d6	4/4

ARKANNAD

This barbarian scout is a strange individual and the most complex of these Non-Player Characters.

Arkannad is 29 years old, large (183 centimetres, 92 kilograms), and well built. He moves like a cat and is even stronger than he looks. Despite his raw vitality, he is not attractive—not ugly in any simple sense, but off-putting. His intense brown eyes are a little too close together, his long brown hair matted into dreadlocks, his beard unkempt, and his body odour oppressive. Worse, though, is his personality: Arkannad is taciturn, distant, and not personable. The overall impression is that he is nearly feral. His prized possession is a handsome, long bear skin that protects his back and much of his torso; great bear claw arms dangle over the shoulders in front, with the attached head acting as a helmet. His limbs remain bare, for mobility. From his strong accent, an adventurer could glean that he is not from Advent, but he will sound like any barbarians they meet to the south.

He is a vagabond from the Kirstet clan, whose homeland is to the north in the stretch of land between the hills and the Southvale River, and who have a reputation for toughness and violence. This explains some (but not all) of his odd demeanour. In fact, Arkannad was nearly as unpopular amongst his own people as he is amongst these civilised folk—one reason he took up the solitary profession of frontier explorer. Six months ago, his curiosity got the better of him and he entered Advent, to see if civilisation was as strange as he had heard. He does find it strange, but also intriguing, and here he enjoys its manifold distractions and pleasures while being close enough to wilder country to escape as needed.

Arkannad was brought into Zarand's gang by Tobias and remains as his bodyguard. His comrades have welcomed his skills and savage reputation around town, yet do not trust him entirely. He is moderately loyal, but in the end he is too self-involved and quirky to be truly reliable. Despite his difficult personality, most of the time, it is fairly easy to get along with him because he keeps to himself. When he does speak, though, his arrogance and frankness get annoying quickly. He wants to stay in Advent for now, but his wanderlust will resurge. Arkannad's chief personal goal is to see the world; other goals include honing his skills to realise his Inner Beast, spending time alone, and observing absurd civilised customs.

Aside from being antisocial, Arkannad's chief flaw is tempestuousness. He is moody and prone to outbursts, and he does not take insult lightly. He is proud of his abilities and keen to demonstrate them by besting others. He has little patience for the frailties of soft civilised folk who have grown up sleeping in beds. Arkannad's idiom is wildness, undisciplined power, pride, and hostility.

He is a lay worshipper of the Renegade God Renamos, and thus knows Folk Magic, unlike his civilised comrades. His culture also venerates its ancestors, so he respects and fears the dead and the spirit world. His civilised companions deride him as superstitious, hence his Passion of that name. This Passion should be checked at the Haunted Campsite. Defiling a tomb is amongst the most serious taboos of Arkannad's people.

On this quest, Arkannad is not interested in the treasure, but rather in the challenge of obtaining it, and he is obedient to his leader. However, if Tobias were to say the wrong thing and imply that Arkannad were strange for not wanting the loot, or worse still that he were greedy for it, then that would be insulting—and, as mentioned, this barbarian does not deal well with insults. Alienating Arkannad would be a grave mistake for Tobias. Generally, Tobias uses Arkannad's drive to overcome challenges to manipulate him.

Arkannad's immediate plans: Support Tobias, unless it means risking life and limb. Study the adventurers for weaknesses and question everything about them, implying they are inferior. Neutralise Loram as needed to help Tobias or just to prove himself.

He carries all of his personal possessions. For this mission, he bears rope and grapnel, but these actually belong to Tobias. He is quick to boast about getting his bear skin the old-fashioned way during his coming-of-age ritual.

Equipment: Bear skin, shortspear, falchion, hunting knife, hatchet, sling, 5 sling stones, pack, First Aid and Healing kits, firemaker, food, water skin, 20 metres of rope, grapnel, 5 SP (Unburdened)

This barbarian has many skills valuable for this sort of adventure. Note that his Navigation (Open Country) will be applicable in the Wilds, but not in the Dead Swamp. He carries many weapons and is skilled with still more. In combat, Arkannad prefers to start off using his spear, up close or at range, but his falchion may be even more dangerous. He uses his sling only at quite long range.

Characteristics		Attributes		1d20	Location	AP/HP
STR: 16	Action Points		3	1–3	Right Leg	-/6
CON: 13	Damage Modifier		+1d2	4–6	Left Leg	-/6
SIZ: 14	Magic Points		11	7–9	Abdomen	1/7
DEX: 17	Movement		6m	10–12	Chest	1/8
INT: 13	Initiative Bonus		13	13–15	Right Arm	-/5
POW: 11	Armour		Bear skin on torso, bear head helm	16–18	Left Arm	-/5
CHA: 6	Luck Points		2	19–20	Head	5/6
	Folk Magic		27% (Bladesharp, Might)			

Skills: Acrobatics 43%, Athletics 81%, Boating 29%, Brawn 53%, Conceal 28%, Culture (Civilised Frontier) 31%, Customs 66%, Dance 23%, Deceit 19%, Drive 28%, Endurance 74%, Evade 50%, First Aid 40%, Folk Magic 27%, Healing 29%, Influence 12%, Insight 24%, Locale 36%, Lore (Animals) 31%, Native Tongue 59%, Navigation (Open Country) 47%, Perception 63%, Ride 33%, Sing 17%, Stealth 54%, Survival 47%, Swim 39%, Track 31%, Unarmed 48%, Willpower 32%

Passions: Loyal to Clan 74%, Superstitious about the Dead 64%, Antisocial 59%, Easily Offended 54%

Combat Style: Kirstet Villager (Battleaxe, Club, Dagger, Sling) 54%, Kirstet Scout (Shortspear, Hatchet, Sling; Swashbuckling) 68%

Weapon	Size/Force	Reach	Damage	AP/HP
Dagger	S	S	1d4+1+1d2	6/8
Club	M	M	1d6+1d2	4/4
Hatchet	S	S	1d6+1d2	3/6
Shortspear	M	L	1d8+1+1d2	4/5
Battle Axe	M	M	1d6+1+1d2	4/8
Sling	L	-	1d8+1d2	1/2

FINIEL

This talented but self-centred woman has long light brown hair, large blue eyes, and pale skin. She is both attractive and personable—and knows it. At 26 years old, she has the lean muscularity of a dancer (60 kilograms), is slightly tall for a woman (173 centimetres), and is very coordinated. Though her looks are distinctive, she uses a myriad of simple disguises (scarves, shawls, an eye patch, mud, a walking stick, etc.) to make herself less conspicuous as desired.

Finiel is reckless and enjoys bantering and lampooning people. Usually she is not mean, but she can be, as she has a sharp temper. She has worked hard to become patient, but prefers acting to waiting, and is irritated more than the average person by boredom and inactivity. She is not adept at flirting, but makes friends very easily, telling jokes and smiling a lot. Often she uses her other talents to avoid being noticed at all so she can watch people, one of her favourite pastimes. At heart, she is a social creature (just not very trusting) and strongly prefers town life to exploring The Wilds.

She grew up as an urchin on the streets of Advent and so has not followed any traditional path towards a career or marriage. Her circumstances have rendered her a fair pickpocket, burglar, and spy. Finiel does not remember her parents, nor does she think much about them. While she is no scholar, her intelligence and penchant for eavesdropping have garnered her decent knowledge of local history and current events. She is even a bit literate.

For seven years, Zarand has been a father figure to Finiel and has put her talents to good use. Her job in the gang has been to keep an eye out about town, pilfering here and there, identifying easy marks, and otherwise acquiring bits of information. However, as the scenario unfolds, she realises that her prospects in Advent are now extremely limited. After this last big job, Finiel intends to leave town for greener pastures in Cylder. Her talents should help her to get a job with Kardesh Weathervane, which would also protect her from Tobias (as she has gleaned from rare remarks she has overheard). Her chief personal goals are to acquire money and luxury, and to have some fun.

Her chief flaw is that she is exploitative. She might ditch her friends in a pinch to save her own skin, or to attain some great profit. She walks away from relationships rather than making amends. Finiel's idiom is stealth and self-interest, with wit and charm. She will make a solid adventurer—if she lasts long enough.

Finiel's immediate plans: Watch Tobias like a hawk, wait for an opening, and pay him back for killing Zarand. Get as much treasure as possible. If necessary, abandon anyone to his fate—even Loram. Get out of Advent.

She wears quilted armour, a shortsword, a dagger concealed at her back and another in her right boot, and a sling with its bullets in her pocket. Her money and inessential items like disguises have been left in Advent. She is happy to let Loram carry her bulkier stuff.

Equipment: Armour, short sword, 2 daggers, sling, 8 bullets, pack, First Aid kit, water skin, rations, thief's toolkit, 10 m rope, grapnel, lantern, 5 candles, firemaker, large sack, thin silver bracelet (Unburdened)

Finiel fights bravely, but she is not very tough in close combat. She is more effective at range with her sling. As mentioned, she wants revenge for Zarand's death and so will attack Tobias at the most opportune moment, late in the adventure, without flinching.

Characteristics	Attributes		1d20	Location	AP/HP
STR: 11	Action Points	3	1–3	Right Leg	2/5
CON: 13	Damage Modifier	None	4–6	Left Leg	2/5
SIZ: 12	Magic Points	12	7–9	Abdomen	2/6
DEX: 16	Movement	6m	10–12	Chest	2/7
INT: 15	Initiative Bonus	14	13–15	Right Arm	2/4
POW: 12	Armour	Quilted	16–18	Left Arm	2/4
CHA: 13	Luck Points	2	19–20	Head	2/5
	Folk Magic	None			

Skills: Athletics 61%, Brawn 23%, Commerce 38%, Conceal 33%, Customs 70%, Deceit 48%, Disguise 39%, Endurance 41%, Evade 62%, First Aid 31%, Influence 56%, Insight 42%, Literacy 35%, Lore (Local History) 35%, Native Tongue 78%, Perception 67%, Sleight 54%, Stealth 71%, Streetwise 75%, Swim 24%, Unarmed 27%, Willpower 44%

Passions: Selfish 75%, Vengeful 66%, Covets Wealth 54%

Combat Style: *Frontier Rogue (Shortsword, Club, Buckler, Short Bow; Swashbuckling) 37%, Frontier Commoner (Hatchet, Dagger, Sling) 42%*

Weapon	Size/Force	Reach	Damage	AP/HP
Dagger	S	S	1d4+1	6/8
Club	M	M	1d6	4/4
Hatchet	S	S	1d6	3/6
Buckler	M	S	1d3	6/9
Shortsword	M	S	1d6	6/8
Short Bow	L	-	1d6	4/4
Sling	L	-	1d8	1/2

LORAM THE LARGE

This bear of a man is 22 years old, hugely muscular and intimidating (201 centimetres, 154 kilograms), and ungainly. Loram has brown eyes and hair and a ruddy complexion, and is reasonably handsome, though he scowls a lot. He wears his hair and beard long, but unlike Arkannad he is well groomed. Though he is a man of few words, he is not stupid—just quiet. Most of the time, he is happy for Finiel to do the talking. However, he does enjoy taking a turn at storytelling around the campfire, if someone else has broken the ice.

Loram grew up poor in a nearby village up the River Cylder. His parents quickly understood that his physical prowess could earn him a future in the military that candle-making would never match, so they sent him to Advent with best wishes. Despite his humble origins, he was brought up right and is more cultured than one might expect, with training in Courtesy and Customs, and he cannot stand those who break the rules. This causes him much internal conflict, considering his most recent occupation. The only reason he stays with it is to keep a close eye on Finiel and protect her as needed. He is loyal to a fault.

His frustration runs deeper still: Unfortunately, an imagined insult has led to a family feud with the Captain of the Guard, which keeps Loram from joining the garrison. Thus, his main personal goal is to leave Advent for a fresh start in Cylder (or better still Nyren, which by all accounts is much nicer), become a soldier, and serve his king. However, he is smitten with Finiel and does not want to abandon her, especially considering her trouble with Tobias. His other personal goals include improving his combat and other physical skills, advancing in his cult, and becoming a famous and feared warrior (all closely related). He is an Initiate of Sormund and attends services dutifully, travelling all the way to the Temple of the Founding Four in Cylder for holy days.

Loram's idiom is brute force, as expected. His strength is impressive, and handy, and he makes an obvious target—three reasons why the gang keeps him around. An important foible for this adventure is that he is afraid of heights, so he will be quite nervous on the narrow trail up Nameless Hill.

Loram's immediate plans: Support Finiel, even if it means risking life and limb. Crush Tobias like a bug if possible. Stick with Finiel when it is time to leave Advent.

He wears a full suit of lamellar armour and bears a tremendous great hammer, plus two javelins. He carries some weighty gear, but is so strong that he can afford it. He even carries Finiel's bedroll for her. His money and inessential items have been left in Advent.

Equipment: Armour, Great hammer, 2 javelins, pack, 2 bedrolls, 2 water skins, rations, First Aid kit, 2 6-hour torches, firemaker, 2 large sacks (Unburdened)

Loram is the heaviest hitter in this crew. He is definitely the one you want around when fighting, say, a wyvern. If he loses his weapon or is closed upon, he will happily Grapple.

Characteristics	Attributes		1d20	Location	AP/HP
STR: 17	Action Points	2	1–3	Right Leg	4/6
CON: 16	Damage Modifier	+1d4	4–6	Left Leg	4/6
SIZ: 18	Magic Points	11	7–9	Abdomen	4/7
DEX: 9	Movement	6m	10–12	Chest	4/8
INT: 13	Initiative Bonus	6	13–15	Right Arm	4/5
POW: 11	Armour	Lamellar	16–18	Left Arm	4/5
CHA: 9	Luck Points	2	19–20	Head	4/6
	Folk Magic	None			

Skills: *Athletics 41%, Brawn 65%, Courtesy 27%, Customs 71%, Endurance 57%, Evade 32%, First Aid 32%, Gambling 27%, Insight 44%, Lore (Strategy & Tactics) 31%, Lore (Military History) 50%, Perception 39%, Streetwise 40%, Survival 32%, Swim 33%, Unarmed 56%, Willpower 52%*

Passions: *Hate Oath Breakers, Smitten with Finiel 55%, Loyal to King Myur and The Vale 54%, Fear of Heights 52%*

Combat Style: *Frontier Skullcrusher (Great Hammer, Great Club, Military Flail, Javelin; Skirmishing) 61%*

Weapon	Size/Force	Reach	Damage	AP/HP
Great Hammer	H	L	1d10+3+1d4	4/10
Javelin	H	-	1d8+1+1d4	3/8

BARBARIANS

These clan warriors are young (about 22) and eager to prove themselves. They are wild and brave and use deadly force, but flee per their assignment if they sustain worse than Minor Wounds. These youngsters have not been trained to fight from horseback; their mounts are used only for transportation. A quick escape should be easy if things go wrong for them. Unlike civilised folk, these barbarians worship Renamos and know a little Folk Magic, relevant to combat.

Equipment: Armour, Battleaxe, Buckler, 2 javelins, hatchet, haversack, water skin, firemaker, First Aid kit (Unburdened)

Characteristics	Attributes		1d20	Location	AP/HP
STR: 12	Action Points	2	1–3	Right Leg	1/5
CON: 11	Damage Modifier	None	4–6	Left Leg	1/5
SIZ: 13	Magic Points	10	7–9	Abdomen	1/6
DEX: 10	Movement	6m	10–12	Chest	1/7
INT: 13	Initiative Bonus	9	13–15	Right Arm	1/4
POW: 10	Armour	Fur and Hides	16–18	Left Arm	1/4
CHA: 10	Luck Points	2	19–20	Head	1/5
	Folk Magic	25% (Bladesharp)			

Skills: Athletics 67%, Boating 23%, Brawn 70%, Conceal 20%, Customs 66%, Dance 20%, Deceit 23%, Drive 20%, Endurance 67%, Evade 50%, First Aid 33%, Folk Magic 25%, Influence 20%, Insight 23%, Locale 46%, Lore (Strategy & Tactics) 31%, Native Tongue 63%, Navigation (Open Country) 28%, Perception 48%, Ride 35%, Sing 20%, Stealth 38%, Survival 31%, Swim 23%, Track 29%, Unarmed 52%, Willpower 20%

Passions: Loyal to Clan Chieftain 55%, Likes to Fight 53%, Hate Interlopers 53%

Combat Style: Clan Warrior (Battleaxe, Hatchet, Buckler, Javelin; Skirmishing) 62%

Weapon	Size/Force	Reach	Damage	AP/HP
Buckler	M	S	1d3	6/9
Hatchet	S	S	1d6	3/6
Javelin	H	-	1d8+1	3/8
Battleaxe	M	M	1d6+1	4/8

VENOMOUS SNAKES

These serpents resemble the water moccasin, reaching lengths over 2 metres. They are larger than the Marsh Vipers and Moor Vipers described in *Book of Quests*, though their venom is less dangerous. They are not especially aggressive and will attack a large animal or human only defensively, preferring to hide or flee. The biggest problem is stepping on or near one by accident. They can move quickly, but mostly lie very still and may get to attack by surprise. A snake needs to use the Inject Venom special effect to poison a victim (MYTHRAS, page 218), but its bite does not need to do damage to accomplish this.

Note that a character should be penalised one grade when attacking such a small creature.

Swamp Snake Venom

- Application: Injection
- Potency: 50%
- Resistance: Endurance
- Onset time: 1d3+1 minutes
- Duration: 1d2 days

Conditions: The victim feels Agony in the wounded location after 2 rounds (almost immediately), then Nausea at onset time, followed by Confusion and Exhaustion in about 30 minutes. Death occurs only rarely, due to anaphylaxis (decided at Games Master's fiat).

Antidote/Cure: A generic snakebite medicine would be effective, if anyone should have some. The Healing skill can prevent further symptoms from appearing, but cannot prevent the Agony and Nausea.

Characteristics	Attributes		1d20	Location	AP/HP
STR: 4	Action Points	3	1–2	Tail Tip	1/2
CON: 7	Damage Modifier	-1d8	3–10	End-length	1/2
SIZ: 1	Magic Points	4	11–18	Fore-length	1/3
DEX: 17	Movement	6m (Land and Swimming)	19–20	Head	1/2
INS: 12	Initiative Bonus	15			
POW: 4	Armour	Scales			
	Abilities	Cold Blooded, Dark Sight, Swimmer, Venomous			

Skills: *Athletics 71%, Brawn 45%, Endurance 54%, Evade 74%, Perception 56%, Stealth 69%, Swim 51%, Willpower 28%*

Combat Style: *Scaly Fiend (Bite) 61%*

Weapon	Size/Force	Reach	Damage	AP/HP
Bite	S	T	1d3-1d8	As for Head

COYOTES

These canids are essentially wolves, for game purposes, except that they are smaller and weaker—and faster and sneakier. (The members of this particular pack are slightly smarter and more coordinated than average.) They are not as aggressive as wolves, their packs are smaller and not as rigidly hierarchical, and they tend more towards scavenging and an omnivorous diet. In this scenario, they are interested in making off with the party's food. A coyote does not attack an adventurer unless it absolutely cannot run away. If it does attack, it uses the same tactics as a wolf: Grip and Choose Location (exposed area), with on-going damage to a Gripped location.

Characteristics	Attributes		1d20	Location	AP/HP
STR: 4	Action Points	3	1–2	Right Hind Leg	1/3
CON: 11	Damage Modifier	-1d6	3–4	Left Hind Leg	1/3
SIZ: 4	Magic Points	7	5–7	Hindquarters	1/4
DEX: 12	Movement	10m	8–10	Forequarters	1/5
INS: 14	Initiative Bonus	13	11–13	Right Front Leg	1/3
POW: 7	Armour	Fur	14–16	Left Front Leg	1/3
	Abilities	Night Sight	17–20	Head	1/3

Skills: *Athletics 56%, Brawn 28%, Endurance 62%, Evade 64%, Perception 61%, Stealth 66%, Track 55%, Willpower 34%*

Passions: *Be the Leader of the Pack 60%, Scavenge 90%*

Combat Style: *Trickster Savage (Bite) 56%*

Weapon	Size/Force	Reach	Damage	AP/HP
Bite	S	T	1d4-1d6	As for Head

Swamp Devils

These variant earth elementals are inimical to intruders. Each attacks by surprise to engulf a randomly chosen adventurer (but a mule or horse is too big). This particular variety of gnome is made of mud, not gravelly earth, and is a bit below average in Strength and HP and does less damage, but its engulfed victim could suffocate (Mythras, page 71). It can also Sling Mud at range, and neither runs out of ammunition nor needs to spend time reloading.

Characteristics	Attributes		1d20	Location	AP/HP
STR: 14	Action Points	2	1–20	Body	1/15
DEX: 7	Damage Modifier	+1d2			
INS: 9	Magic Points	10			
POW: 10	Movement	6m			
SIZ: 2 cubic metres	Initiative Bonus	8			
	Armour	1 pt of Protection vs. magical damage; Immune to non-magical weapons			
	Abilities	Engulfing, Suffocation, Immunity (Earth attacks), Vulnerable (Air attacks)			

Skills: Brawn 48%, Evade 54%, Perception 49%, Willpower 70%

Passions: Protect Territory 85%

Combat Style: Elemental Fury (Smash, Sling Mud, Engulf) 61%

Weapon	Size/Force	Reach	Damage	AP/HP
Smash	M	M	1d2+1d2	As for Body
Sling Mud	L	-	1d2	-
Engulf	M	M	1d2 to every location	-

Haunts of the Campsite

Each of these many spirits is Intensity 1 and has either the Glamour or Miasma magical ability.

Characteristics	Attributes		1d20	Location	AP/HP
INT: 13	Action Points	2	1–20	Body	1/15
POW: 9	Initiative Bonus	12			
CHA: 10	Magic Points/Hit Points	9			
	Movement	6m			
	Abilities	Manifest, plus Either Glamour (sight or sound) or Miasma			

Skills: Brawn Willpower 70%

Passions: Inflict Fear 85%

Wyverns of the Misty Falls

Such a beast swoops in from above, fighting from the air unless such becomes impossible. It will charge through contact, using either of its attacks. Its tail sweep enjoys the Bash special effect and might affect more than one character, being a Sweep attack (MYTHRAS, page 105).

A wyvern has both grasping and incising teeth, so when biting it may choose from the special effects Grip, Impale, or Bleed. It prefers to Grip a character, use Brawn in a contest of strength to lift her off the hillside and then drop her to her doom.

If either of its wings takes damage approaching a Serious Wound, a wyvern disengages and flies off. Of course, if either wing is reduced to 0 HP, then the monster must land—above the party on the crumbling hillside, if at all possible. If it is still not badly hurt aside from its wing, it continues to fight, until just before it is seriously hurt in a key location (Head, Forequarters, or Hindquarters).

Characteristics	Attributes		1d20	Location	AP/HP
STR: 27	Action Points	3	1–3	Tail	6/12
CON: 18	Damage Modifier	+1d8+1d6	4–5	Right Hind Leg	6/13
SIZ: 45	Magic Points	11	6–7	Left Hind Leg	6/13
DEX: 18	Movement	8m (Land) 16m (Flying)	8–10	Hindquarters	6/14
INS: 13	Initiative Bonus	16	11–14	Forequarters	6/15
POW: 11	Armour	Scales	15–16	Right Wing	6/13
	Abilities	Cold Blooded, Dark Sight, Flying, Frenzy	17–18	Left Wing	6/13
			19–20	Head	6/14

Skills: *Athletics 65%, Brawn 90%, Endurance 80%, Evade 70%, Fly 75%, Perception 65%, Willpower 65%*

Passions: *Protect Territory 90%, Feed 80%*

Combat Style: *Draconic Terror (Bite, Tail Sweep) 85%*

Weapon	Size/Force	Reach	Damage	AP/HP
Bite	E	L	1d12+1d8+1d6	As for Head
Tail Sweep	E	VL	1d10+1d8+1d6	As for Tail

Skeleton Guardians

These are the skeletons of Grestet warriors who were, on average, a bit bigger, stronger, healthier, and more coordinated than the average human. They are animated by Intensity 2 Spirits of Undeath, bound to the Head hit location.

Their armour is stained with age, but the leather straps have fared well, due to the moist cave air yet absence of mould. Note that although they do not carry their own, the skeletons know how to wield spears, if such become available during combat.

Remember that skeletons are vulnerable to blunt-trauma weapons (raise damage dice one step), but resistant to slashing (reduce one step) and thrusting (reduce two steps) weapons. Those modifiers also apply to falling and stake damage, if anyone is clever enough to push a skeleton into the pit.

Characteristics	Attributes		1d20	Location	AP/HP
STR: 12	Action Points	3	1–3	Right Leg	0/6
CON: 12	Damage Modifier	+1d2	4–6	Left Leg	0/6
SIZ: 14	Magic Points	14	7–9	Abdomen	5/7
DEX: 17	Movement	6m	10–12	Chest	5/8
INT: 13	Initiative Bonus	13	13–15	Right Arm	0/5
POW: 14	Armour	Hoplite Plate Cuirass and Helm	16–18	Left Arm	0/5
	Abilities	Undead	19–20	Head	5/6

Skills: *Athletics 69%, Brawn 46%, Endurance 44%, Evade 74%, Perception 57%, Unarmed 69%, Willpower 68%*

Passions: *Protect the Treasure Hoard 100%*

Combat Style: *Skeletal Guardian (Broadsword, Longspear, Hoplite Shield) 69%*

Weapon	Size/Force	Reach	Damage	AP/HP
Hoplite Shield	H	S	1d4	6/15
Broadsword	M	M	1d8+1d2	6/10
Longspear	L	L	1d10+1d2	6/12

www.ingramcontent.com/pod-product-compliance
Ingram Content Group UK Ltd.
Pitfield, Milton Keynes, MK11 3LW, UK
UKHW050459150426
5217IPUK00025B/1754